The Hole in the Heart of God

The Hole in the Heart of God

—— Stories of Creation and Redemption ——

Paul K. Hooker

RESOURCE *Publications* · Eugene, Oregon

THE HOLE IN THE HEART OF GOD
Stories of Creation and Redemption

Copyright © 2021 Paul K. Hooker. All rights reserved. Except for brief quotations in critical publications or reviews, no part of this book may be reproduced in any manner without prior written permission from the publisher. Write: Permissions, Wipf and Stock Publishers, 199 W. 8th Ave., Suite 3, Eugene, OR 97401.

Resource Publications
An Imprint of Wipf and Stock Publishers
199 W. 8th Ave., Suite 3
Eugene, OR 97401

www.wipfandstock.com

PAPERBACK ISBN: 978-1-7252-9972-6
HARDCOVER ISBN: 978-1-7252-9973-3
EBOOK ISBN: 978-1-7252-9974-0

06/10/21

"The Second Day" and "I Seek the Shining Darkness" were previously published in *Days and Times: Poems from the Liturgy of Living*, by Paul K. Hooker. Resource Publications: Eugene OR, 2018.

All Scripture quotations are from New Revised Standard Version Bible, copyright © 1989 National Council of the Churches of Christ in the United States of America. Used by permission. All rights reserved worldwide.

Cover image: A simulated view of a black hole, created by Hotaka Shiokawa. Used by permission of the artist.

To David F. White
Colleague, friend, kindred spirit
Fellow traveler in realms of Fire and Beauty

Lead us up beyond unknowing and light,
Up to the farthest, highest peak
Of mystic scripture,
Where the mysteries of God's Word
Lie simple, absolute, and unchangeable
in the brilliant darkness of a hidden silence.

—Pseudo-Dionysius the Areopagite, *Mystical Theology,* 1.1

Contents

Introduction | ix

Poems: The Hole in the Heart of God: A Paschal Vigil in Poetry | 3

    Fire

    Prelude: Elijah Calls Down Fire   *Fire* | 3

    Word

I.	A World is Created	*The Hole in the Heart of God I* | 7
II.	Love Floods the World	*Light Falls* | 10
III.	Isaac is Bound	*The Knife* | 12
IV.	Israel is Delivered at the Sea	*The Crossing I* | 14
V.	The Words are Given to Moses on the Mountain	*Children's Sermon* | 17
VI.	The Spies are Concealed by Rahab	*The Crimson Cord* | 20
VII.	Samuel Encounters God	*The Call* | 22
VIII.	The Song of the Vineyard	*Confession* | 25
IX.	The Valley of the Bones	*I Seek the Shining Darkness* | 27
X.	Jonah in the Belly of the Beast	*The Belly of the Beast* | 29
XI.	Jesus is Alienated from the Father	*The Hole in the Heart of God II* | 31
XII.	Resurrection	*Resurrection* | 34

CONTENTS

Water

The Crossing II | 37

Meal

The Invitation | 39

Illumining Fire | 41

Ruminations

Fire | 45

'Ein Sof—The Infinite | 49

Sefirot—The Ten Names of God | 52

Light and Desire | 56

Tzimtzum—The Hole in the Heart of God | 60

Love and Judgment | 63

Divided Seas | 67

Holy Deserts, Holy Mountains | 72

Cloud and Fire and Glory | 78

The Cord | 82

Shevirah—The Shattering | 87

The Shining Darkness | 92

Atonement—The Hole in the Heart of God | 97

Tikkun—Light, Love, Repair | 102

Shekinah—Presence | 106

Postscript: Method and Imagination | 109

Introduction

Each Holy Saturday, Christians gather at twilight for a paschal vigil that awaits the dawn of Easter Day. They set a new fire, and from that fire light the paschal candle that will burn in the sanctuary throughout the coming year. They read passages of Scripture that recount God's engagement with the world from creation through the crucifixion to the resurrection, a story of brokenness and redemption, alienation and reconciliation. The vigil concludes with the baptism of new converts to the faith and the celebration of the Eucharist. The vigil is ancient, reaching back into the earliest days of the Church, but is still practiced in Christian communities. Through the myth of the vigil, past and future are gathered into the mystery of the present.

Judaism, too, has its mythic reflection on God's engagement with creation and redemption. Kabbalah, the great tradition of Jewish mystical speculation, holds that in the eternal moment before creation *'Ein Sof*, the Infinite One who is all in all, withdraws or contracts so that a space might come into being where all that is not the Infinite One might exist, a sort of "hole" in the being of God. Like the Christian paschal readings, Kabbalah tells the story of creation, brokenness and redemption, alienation and reconciliation. Like the vigil, Kabbalah gathers past and future into the mystical present.

Myth, especially religious myth, has a peculiar power to explain the world. Myth also has power to enchant the world, to loosen the stranglehold of post-Enlightenment rationalism and free the imagination. I am convinced that the great myths of religious experience are true in the way that great art or poetry is true. They invite me into a knowing that transcends factuality and requires no proof. I think that all the stories of the great faith traditions are myths, including the stories of my own faith.

The similarity between these two great mythic retellings of the sacred story is not accidental. Both are influenced by the same sources: the stories and poems of Hebrew Scripture and the speculative work of

INTRODUCTION

neo-platonic philosophers of the three Abrahamic traditions in the period between the 2nd and 12th centuries CE. Throughout this period and beyond, Christian and Jewish mystics, as well as later Muslim mystics in the Sufi tradition, borrowed concepts and recast ideas from each other to their own purposes, mutually interpreting one another in an ever-rising crescendo of wonder and awe.

The poems and ruminations in this book are intended as a continuation of that process of mutual reinterpretation. They are not an effort to evacuate the meaning of one tradition and replace it with the content of the other. Rather, they are an effort to read both Scripture and tradition in a different and imaginative way (more about this in the Postscript). At least as I imagine them, these poems and ruminations are a sort of conversation between the two great mythic traditions of Judaism and Christianity.

The poems are presented as a paschal vigil, each corresponding to a passage from Hebrew Scripture (and two from the New Testament). As the vigil progresses through the four parts—Fire, Word, Water, and Meal—the readings tell the story of God's engagement with the world from creation to redemption. Paired with each reading is a poem that reflects on that reading, and a poetic prayer. Liturgical directions are provided so that the readings and poems might be used as the text for a paschal vigil. Those who use these poems in a vigil are strongly encouraged to read the entire scriptural text for each poem, and not merely the epigraph that appears herein.

The ruminations are intended as a sort of larger context for the poems. They are an effort to explore themes and motifs that appear in the poems in more or less the order of appearance, but not to explain the poems or restrict the range of meaning that may occur to the reader. The term "rumination" evokes for me the behavior of a ruminant, a deer in a forest clearing or a cow in a pasture, following its nose from one tasty mouthful of grass to another, completely absorbed in the nourishment it receives. These ruminations are not academic essays or formal interpretations of biblical texts; rather they are mystical "grazings" in the cool woodland clearings and rich sunlit pastures of the text. The ruminations might be effectively used as starting points for conversations about both the texts and the poems in a forum for discussion at some point after the vigil.

Both the poems and the ruminations draw on both Christian and Jewish mysticism (especially Kabbalah) as they reflect on the text, in something of the same way as early Christian commentaries reflected on both Old and New Testaments, and as the Talmud reflects on the Torah.

INTRODUCTION

While the setting is explicitly Christian, it is the intent of this work to illustrate poetically the power of myths mutually to inform each other, creating thereby a new experience of thought or worship, enhancing each with the infusion of the other.

In the end, though, I claim both poems and ruminations as my own, without imprimatur of either tradition. They are the palaces of my imagination, built using the stones left behind by others who once erected palaces of their own. I have wandered through their ruined, mythic halls in wide-eyed awe at their beauty and intricacy, their imaginative possibility whose surface I have only barely scratched. These musings of mine are no match for theirs, and they are impermanent. Eventually, time brings to ruin all human edifices, real or imagined, leaving their remnants to serve as the cornerstones of others. Only the myths endure.

Poems

The Hole In the Heart of God

A Paschal Vigil in Poetry

"An act of creation is possible only through 'the entry of God into Himself,' that is, through the act of tzimtzum, *whereby ['Ein Sof] contracts Himself and so makes it possible for something which is not 'Ein Sof to exist. Some part of the Godhead therefore withdraws and leaves room, so to speak, for the creative processes to come into play."*—Gershom Scholem[1]

FIRE

[*The vigil begins in darkness. All gather in silence around the fire-pit. Each participant is given a small, unlit candle.*]

Prelude: Elijah Calls Down Fire

[*In the darkness, 1Kgs 18:20–39 is read.*]

"Then the fire of the Lord fell and consumed the burnt offering, the wood, the stones, and the dust, and even licked up the water that was in the trench. When all the people saw it, they fell on their faces and said, 'The Lord indeed is God; the Lord indeed is God'" (1 Kgs 18:38–39).

Fire

We limp the circled orgy 'round the fire-ring,
and wager all our life and love on Ba'al.
O, fire the wood, consume the offering!
In vain we pray the lightning bolt to fall.

---

1. Gershom Sholem, *Kabbalah*. New York: Quadrangle. 1974, p. 129.

A little proof is all we seek: enough
to justify our shared presumptive truth,
a solace when the going gets too rough,
excuse for wary eye and bloody tooth.

Yet neither lightning falls nor fire consumes,
though surely prayers are fervid, true, and pure,
and hearts are set on all that heart presumes,
feet follow in the dance while strength endures.

But see that other altar, silent token
of the Strange One, full of cloud and storm,
whose name by tongue has never yet been spoken,
whose will bespeaks a world 'ere it takes form.

Whence comes this One, this Older-Than-the-Stones,
who counts the glassy grains along the strand
and knows the language written in the bones
beneath the skin of mountains where we stand?

Go back, go back, before there is until;
melt the rocks, evaporate the seas,
put out the stars, and bid the wind be still—
'til Light is all that only Light can see.

Antiphon in the Darkness

O Light!
            But how can there be light, if there is no darkness?
O Endless!
            But how can there be no end if there is no beginning?

O Only!
>   **But how can there be only if there is no other?**

O Truth!
>   **But how can there be truth if there is no falsehood?**

O All!
>   **But how can there be all if there is no any?**

'Ein Sof—The Infinite

We who *are* cannot in mind portray
what *is* before any *is* commence.
We who speak have not the words to say
that might connote the sound of sheerest Silence.

We peer into the blackness of the Light
but cannot see all that cannot be seen.
We yearn to know but know we have no right.
Is there a will, and in the will, a dream,

and in the dream a vision of a space,
and in the space a coming into being,
still a synapse in the mind of Grace,
still a sight not yet prepared for seeing?

Light imagines darkness. The One-in-All
summons forth a single blinding star.
Bright as the sun, thin as a hair, it falls
from past the ancient orbs. It is new Fire.

[*The new fire is lit.*]

In the beginning was the Word,
and the Word was with God,
and the Word was God.

The life of Christ is the light of all people.
The light shines in the darkness,
and the darkness will not overcome it.

Prayer:

Come, Fire of Christ, illumine darkness.
Come, Light, and show the way;
Come, Word of Christ, help us to harken
to the words the Light will say.
Through dark of sorrow
to dawn of morrow
O thought of hope, O coming day,
shine on us your eternal ray.

[*The paschal candle is lit from the new fire, and participants' candles from the paschal candle.*]

[*The procession into the sanctuary begins, led by the bearer of the paschal candle.*]

[*As the procession moves forward, the leader and people sing or say responsively:*
The Light of Christ. Thanks be to God.]

WORD

[Hymns and other music may be interspersed between poems and prayers, or after prayers and before readings.]

I. A World is Created

[Gen 1:1–5 is read.]

"In the beginning when God created the heavens and the earth, the earth was a formless void and darkness covered the face of the deep, while a wind from God swept over the face of the waters. Then God said, 'Let there be light; and there was light" (Gen 1:1–3).

The Hole in the Heart of God I

In the beginning was Desire,
and Desire was with The Infinite,
and Desire was The Infinite.
Desire was the crown The Infinite wore,
and Desire made The Infinite Beautiful.

And Desire said, Let there be.
But Wisdom said,
How can there be if there is no room for being?
How can there be *not*, if The Infinite is All in All?
How can *being* be?

Then Understanding said,
Let us cease to be not-being

so that an empty place might be
> where there is no *where* before,
> when there is no before or after,
> while there is neither yes nor no.

Let us make a single point within
> The Infinite
> that is not The Infinite,
> an end where endlessness ends
> and endings begin.

Let it be dark,
> yet yearn for Light.

Let it be grotesque,
> yet seek after Beauty

Let it be hopeless,
> yet full of Desire.

Let it be the place
> where Desire imagines creation.

The Infinite inhaled,
> and became infinitesimally
> smaller, withdrawing,
> fullness contracting
> into lesser full-
> ness, and giv-
> ing birth to
> nothing. A
> creation is
> born

> .

Desire makes a hole in the heart of God.

Desire gives birth to God and not-God.

And God says, Let there be Light.

[*A brief silence is kept.*]

Prayer:

How lovely, Christ, the Emptiness
by which is heaven adorned;
How lovely, Christ, the Timelessness
that dwells before the dawn
before the Light
makes end of night
and signals new creation's morn
wherein the inkling world is born.

II. Love Floods the World

[Gen 6:9–22 is read.]

> "Make yourself an ark of cypress wood . . . For my part, I am going to bring a flood of waters on the earth, to destroy from under heaven all flesh in which is the breath of life; everything that is on the earth shall die. But I will establish my covenant with you . . ."(Gen 6:14, 17–18).

Light Falls

And God desires Light.
So Love floods, explodes upon creation:
    Fireworks sun: novae, nebulae,
    constellations gyre in eternal dance,
    star-cloud towers space-scrape The Infinite,
    a universe expanding, quivers
    pure with fired and sparkled Love.
Light torrents from clouds of glory,
    swells from wellsprings of the deep,
    creation washes, tumbles, drowns
in the whelming Light:
Omnis ad majorem gloriam Dei.

And Love says, Let there be no end to Love,
    as there is no end to endlessness.

No, says Judgment.
Let Love be limited, let there be
    a hope for all that might yet be.
For the traveler always seeks return,
    as the not-God seeks God,
    and emptiness yearns for filling.
Rather let there be form, a boat atop the flood
    and deep within its hold,
    hope and heartache, pain and possibility,
    a pair of every kind—
adrift, through calm and squall,
    with all creation in its womb,
    and never come to shore
    until Love and Judgment are as one
    in the hole in the heart of God.

And God says, Let there be a world amid the waters.

[*A brief silence is kept.*]

Prayer:

O Arc of Light above the mountains
bent low to touch the earth,
O Promise made that stops the fountains
and teaches us our worth,
Praise flight of Dove,
Praise saving Love,
Praise colored bow 'cross heaven's girth,
Praise ark of wood, that holds new birth!

III. Isaac is Bound

[*Gen 22:1–18 is read.*]

"Then Abraham reached out his hand and took the knife to kill his son" (Gen 22:10).

The Knife

Love is the father put to the test,
Judgment the son he holds to his breast.
Beauty is the blade of the knife.

Love is the father righteous and good,
Judgment the son who carries the wood.
Beauty is the blade of the knife.

Love is the father who pauses for rest,
Judgment the son who begs of the quest.
Beauty replies with the knife.

Love, says the father, will surely provide.
Judgment the son who must now decide
if Beauty resides in the knife.

Love is the arm that raises its hand.
Judgment the blood spilled out on the land
by the Beautiful blade of the knife.

What is this Love that kills its own son?
What Judgment stands by for the deed to be done?
What Beauty in the blade of a knife?

Love without Judgment is the love of a fool.
Unloving Judgment vindictive and cruel.
Beauty unites in the knife.

[*A brief silence is kept.*]

Prayer:

O Christ, your love will know no bound;
'tis blood of our redemption.
O Christ, your judgment spills to ground;
'tis our one boon exemption.
Our weak obedience
is but expedience
and nothing more than our convention.
We live by Beauty's intervention.

IV. Israel is Delivered at the Sea

[*Ex 14:10–31 is read.*]

"Then Moses stretched out his hand over the sea. The Lord drove the sea back by a strong east wind all night and turned the sea into dry land; and the waters were divided. The Israelites went into the sea on dry ground, the waters forming a wall for them on their right and on their left" (Ex 14:21–22).

The Crossing I

We who wait in darkness huddled,
terrored by the angel's wings,
have learned to hoard our hope, befuddled,
for want of grander schemes of things.

Blood of lamb and blood of child
mingled in some ghastly plan
in which some die, and some, beguiled,
survive. We had no choice. We ran.

But now at edge of ruthless water,
surrender hope; we wait the fate
of any slave, or son or daughter
of a vast, unyielding state.

POEMS—WORD

Antiphon for the Seashore

O Horse!
        Your hooves pound like pulse of sin.

O Chariot!
        Your wheels grind out a reckoning.

O Sea!
        Your basin bounds both death and life.

O Wave!
        You drown the prayers of desperate strife.

O Rod!
        You limn the path through parted wave.

O Fire!
        You burn, and aught is left to save.

Dare we pass through gathered surge,
a sea divided, torn in twain
at beck of god or demiurge,
transgress the waters deep as pain

toward deserts lit by midnight moon
and mountaintops too high for hope
and promise made but broken soon
and suffering beyond the scope

of words? If we but yield our trust
and pass through waters parted here
will crossing somehow make of us
a people loved and god-endeared?

Who is this "god?" A presence known
in neither effigy nor name

but in the yearning Fire alone,
a Perseverance none can tame

but only follow in the night
toward destinies baptized by fear
and sanctified by headlong flight
ahead of horse and blade and spear.

Yet even Perseverance yields
to Majesty, and tides obey.
Detritus washes up on fields
along the shore. We turn away

toward the Fire that glows ahead
and follow where its shining, bright
against the inky darkness, leads
toward unseen stations in the night.

[*A brief silence is kept.*]

Prayer:

We pass through waters on the way
to places still but dream,
like those of whom the ancients say:
they trusted things unseen.
Teach us such peace
as may release
our spirits from sin's slav'ry mean,
and drown us all, and make us clean.

V. The Words Are Given to Moses on the Mountain

[*Ex 24:15-18 and Deut 6:1-9 are read.*]

"Then Moses went up on the mountain, and the cloud covered the mountain. The glory of the Lord settled on Mount Sinai, and the cloud covered it for six days."..."Hear, O Israel: The Lord is our God, the Lord alone. You shall love the Lord your God with all your heart, and with all your soul, and with all your might" (Ex 24:15–16; Deut 6:4–5).

Children's Sermon

Listen, little children: I know my hair
smells of burnt wool. I know my eyes
glow with eerie light. Don't be afraid
of me. Glory sometimes does strange things
to a person, if you dare to linger
too long in a place you shouldn't be.

I climbed the mountain, where I shouldn't be.
A wind from someplace ancient stirred my hair,
the smoky air inside the cloud lingered
like a burial shroud wound 'round my eyes,
and I began to be aware of things
moving in the mist. Was I afraid?

The Fire. The Words. I should have been afraid
but there wasn't time. Later there would be
time to think of how It burned up things

I once believed. At the time my hair
seemed to be ablaze, and my eyes
grew bright. I should have run but lingered

while the mountain shook. And now what lingers
in mind is not that I was so afraid
but that I longed to see It eye to eye.
(Of course, I know such things can never be.)
Instead I saw the Fire like silken hair
that danced and shone and burned up everything.

That's what I called you all to hear: that things
are burning. Listen to the Words that linger
on your lips and heart; they singe your hair.
Love the Words, the Fire; yet be afraid.
(To be afraid is what it means to be
wise.) The Fire will sear your shining eyes.

Your shining eyes! Oh, I see in those eyes
the Fire of Glory! It will burn up everything
you love, always causing things to be
reduced to ash and then raised anew. Words linger.
Listen, even though you are afraid;
give all to Love, though Fire ignites your hair.

Children, let it be. Don't close your eyes
or douse your hair. Watch the Fire burn everything.
The One is all that lingers. Be afraid.

[*A brief silence is kept.*]

Prayer:

Teach us the Words not writ in stone
but carved upon the heart;
not scribed upon the stars alone
but known in faith's true art.
Ignite the Fire,
enflame desire
to learn what Love alone imparts:
the One is Light; all else is dark.

VI. The Spies are Concealed by Rahab

[Josh 2:1–21 is read.]

"She said, 'According to your words, so be it.' She sent them away and they departed. Then she tied the crimson cord in the window" (Josh 2:21).

The Crimson Cord

Everything depends upon a crimson cord
hanging in a window, gentled by the breeze.
Everything depends upon these last few words

said in haste, in hope that others will be pleased
to make them true. Everything depends upon
fragile promises made in times like these.

It matters not so much who will have lost or won
as whose promises are kept and whose forgot
and who when all the words are said and deeds are done

spies the crimson cord tied with a faithful knot
to the window and, recalling, stays the sword
and protects this door when the fight grows hot.

Everything depends upon a crimson cord
binding past to hope of what is yet to be:
a home, a place, a life. According to your word

so let it be. Leave now, and on the third of three
cold daybreaks rise and go. Neither pause nor turn
until you reach the future. Yet remember me

and these secrets I have kept that I might earn
a place at table when at last you've kept your word,
and safety in your house, a Fire that, when it burns,

consumes all. From this window like a bird
I would soar, borne aloft by gentle breeze,
no longer tethered here by this crimson cord.

[*A brief silence is kept.*]

Prayer:

Bind us, O Christ of solemn oath,
by cords of love and grace,
that we may yet fulfill this troth
we pledge now in this place.
So let faith stand
with reaching hand
outstretched toward your shining face,
and there your saving love to trace.

VII. Samuel Encounters God

[I Sam 3:1–20 is read.]

"Therefore Eli said to Samuel, 'Go, lie down; and if he calls you, you shall say, "Speak, Lord, for your servant is listening."' So Samuel went and lay down in his place" (1 Sam 3:9).

The Call

It was the Fire—
embodied with a disembodied light
shimmering, quivering against the door—
but what I remember is the smell,
smoke and seared flesh,
some burnt and some about to be.
Holiness, it seems, always smells like that.

I was a boy. I had no name for
how they walked me to the shrine
then turned on heel and headed home.
We're just keeping promises, they said.
These days we'd call it child neglect.
Who brings a child into the world
then abandons him to endless midnights
in empty moonless places, to the clutches
of decrepit priests deafened to the truth
and fickle gods that will not say their name?
No matter. That night, the sum of things
was the Fire it was my job to tend

and a torqued and tangled restless bedsheet
that always seemed to smell of smoke.

Shmuel. God Hears. Nowadays
I chuckle at the too-delicious irony.
They said, this god answers when you ask.
I asked, but heard no answer.
I guess I got the name wrong.

Instead, *Yehoshua,* God Saves, or so
he claimed, when God at long last broke the silence.
Woke me up—arrested my attention—
some tingling of the ear, perhaps some
preternatural cat-like apprehension
of danger waiting just beyond the dawn.
God Hears, God Hears.
The old man said when prompted I should say
I'm listening. Not my will, but thine . . . .

It wasn't so much the sound as the smell:
that piquant Fiery smell of holiness.
Beware of gods who claim they come to save.
Their hot breath torches everything in sight—
temples, priests, nations, thorny crowns,
abandoned sons of men and sons of gods—
'til all that's left behind are the sheets
torqued and tossed aside, or neatly folded:
they always smell of smoke.

Ever since, amid the long *vendette*
between the two competing would-be kings,

'midst petty squabbles over land and women,
a thousand angry neighbors, gesturing
in city gates, and battles sometimes won
but far more often ignominiously lost—
I've tried and mostly failed to save a people
stoutly unconvinced they needed saving.
And still I smell the smoke.

And in the timeless midnights of my life,
wrapped in smoky silence beneath the stars
or else inside an empty, moonless chamber
with stone rolled up and sealed against the holy,
I tend the Fire and listen for our names.
God Hears. God Saves.
Speak, Lord, for thy servant heareth.

[*A brief silence is kept.*]

Prayer:

Teach us to hear in darkness, Lord,
in hours before the light
the awful sound, the fiery word,
the news of coming night;
that with the dawn
we may be strong;
uphold our weakness by your might
and give our souls a measured flight.

VIII. The Song of the Vineyard

[*Isa 5:1–13 is read.*]

" . . . he expected justice,
    but saw bloodshed;
righteousness,
    but heard a cry!" (Isa 5:13).

Confession

Not the misdeed in the dark, the calculated criminality,
not the cynic's act of cruelty, the scandal or the shame. . .
these are not our downfall, Lord, they are clear enough to see;
they offer small temptation to make us break the frame.

But the thousand barely noted little acts of infamy—
small betrayals of the heart, extended hands ignored,
loves dismayed, sleight of poison tongue or stroke of key—
does not each crack the vessel wherein the Light is stored

'til it shatters, and the Light goes skittering
down the swirling darkness that seems to have no end?
We offer heart, we yearn for hope, we raise our voice to sing
songs too faint to call the Light or make it shine again.

You who are the One Light, in whom Desire be found
to make a world the first time: can you not make repair?
You made us; will you not remake us whole and sound
and make a place wherein the act of justice holds our prayer,

'til the world is right, 'til hope does not die a-borning,
and peace no more a stranger in the dark and threatening night?
Then teach our lips and tongues to sing the morning
When even dark shall celebrate the coming of the Light.

Antiphon for the Shattered

O You who made us

                                      See the weakness in your craft

O You who call us

                                      Know we cannot bear to hear

O you who break us

                                      See how all our bones are crushed

O you who bury us

                                      Clothe us with the dust of death

O you who would raise us

                                      Give birth to us in hope.

[*A brief silence is kept.*]

Prayer:

O Christ—who broken on the rood,
with drooping head, stilled heart,
e'en yet repairs, nailed on the wood,
the pain of sinful art—
now from death's lair
the world repair,
rebuild the garden of the good
where once the tree of wisdom stood.

IX. The Valley of the Bones

[*Ezek 37:1–14 is read.*]

"The hand of the Lord came upon me, and he brought me out by the spirit of the Lord and set me down in the middle of a valley; it was full of bones" (Ezek 37:1).

I Seek the Shining Darkness

I seek the shining darkness,
the basement path beneath believing,
the way that knows but is not known.

A voiceless song of echoed longing,
empty skull in an arid vale,
jawbone agape: a windswept moan.

I seek the primordial Before—
before light, or day, or even Word—
region where the Serpent roams,

dragon mother of the deep;
her face the maw of fertile chaos,
her womb is dirt, her breast is bone.

I seek the land of birth and death
from which come both birthing, dying,
to which they go, their labors done,

chthonic realm where little gods
come and go without a sound,
Ultima Thule, wanderer's home.

I seek the dawn of the second day
not the day of witnessed passion
nor when they found the body gone,

but the last pregnant day of possible,
uterus of a new creation,
with cervix of eternal stone.

Deep inside the shining darkness
believing dies and trust, unborn,
unknown and knowing, waits alone.

[*A brief silence is kept.*]

Prayer:

O Christ, in darkness, timeless, waiting
not for release of sunrise
nor rescue, nor for liberating
fire in angelic eyes.
But, quiet, may
then dawn the day
when Light that dark itself denies
awakens in your darkened eyes.

X. Jonah in the Belly of the Beast

[*Jonah 1:17–2:10 is read.*]

"But the Lord provided a large fish to swallow up Jonah; and Jonah was in the belly of the fish three days and three nights. . . . Then the Lord spoke to the fish, and it spewed Jonah out upon the dry land" (Jonah 1:17).

The Belly of the Beast

The darkness is perhaps the place to come to terms
with the craven absence of the Light, the last
fading glimmer of hope, final breath before
the long exhale.

        So this is how it ends, you say:
here in this piscine prison with no possibility
of parole for good behavior. Cell block C
for "Cetacean"—a scholar's joke.

                My crime? Refusing
to go where normal folk would never be caught dead.
Dead. The irony's so thick you could cut it
with a knife. But where's the knife

                        could cut me out
of here? Still, three days swimming in this swamp of hell
will take me where I'd chosen not to go until,
like a bit of cankered meat,

                              death vomits me
onto land. But I've begun this inkling thought:
perhaps my mission here is to prepare the way
for the one who makes this passage

                              after me
whose obedience is stronger than my own,
who will break his body on the waves (or wood—
it's not the medium that matters,

                                        just the message),
and who imagines Light the dark cannot extinguish.
Perhaps the Light will make a passage out. Perhaps
a passage wide enough to allow for two?

[*A brief silence is kept.*]

                         P̲ʀᴀʏᴇʀ:

O Christ, who three days' length did linger
in bowels of the tomb,
O silent voice, O stillèd singer,
yet stillborn in death's womb:
e'en so, we pray,
make yet a way
of rescue from this darkened room.
Unvanquished Light, come Thou, and soon.

XI. Jesus is Alienated from the Father

[*Mark 15:33–39 is read.*]

"When it was noon, darkness came over the whole land until three in the afternoon. At three o'clock Jesus cried out with a loud voice, '*'Eloi, 'Eloi, lemaʿ sabachthani?*' which means, 'My God, my God, why have you forsaken me?'" (Mark 15:34).

The Hole in the Heart of God II

"In the Incarnation, the three show that there is always within God a space that is large enough for the whole world, and even all its sin: The Word's distance from the one he calls Father is so great that no one falls outside it, and the Spirit fills all that space with love." —William C. Placher, *The Triune God: Essays in Postliberal Theology*, p.155

In Silence is Emptiness,

and Emptiness is with Silence,

and Emptiness is Silence.

Emptiness is the womb pregnant with Beauty.

And Emptiness makes Silence Beautiful.

In the eternal moment,

a distance divides their unity

And Emptiness says, Why?

But Silence gives no answer.

And Beauty sees the terror in their eyes.

And Beauty says

THE HOLE IN THE HEART OF GOD

    Let there be a space in Emptiness for Silence.
    Let there be a space in Silence for Emptiness.
See, I dwell in Emptiness and Emptiness is Beautiful.
See, I dwell in Silence and Silence is Beautiful.

This is the hole in the heart of God.
This is the moment of our alienation and our union
    our agony and our joy.

And Silence withdraws
    and becomes eternal and free
        opening a space where
           Emptiness pours
             Itself until
             it is fully
             Empty.

And Beauty says to the caverns of the stars: Come!
        to the rolling canyons of the waves: Come!
          to the Words aloft in the wind: Come!
            to the Fire in the sky: Come!
              to the scattered Light:
                Come!

Come to Emptiness and be filled.
Come to Silence and hear music.
Come to Beauty's Garden and wait.

Come to the doorway of darkness
    to await the gathering of the Light.
Come to the temple of terror

    to await the revelation of Hope.
Come to the cusp of new creation
    to await the birth of Possibility.

Come and wait.

[*A brief silence is kept.*]

Prayer:

O shattered Light, that 'ere poor hours
began their daily race,
be gathered now on Love's rude tower
revealed in time and space;
make all things whole
and heal the soul
that yearns within a world displaced
'til all be one before Love's face.

XII. Resurrection

[Colossians 1:15–20 is read.]

"He is the image of the invisible God, the firstborn
of all creation . . ." (Col 1:16)

Resurrection

Before the dawn, he slips into the flow
so silently no star in heaven hears
nor earth beneath, nor even hell below.
It seems it hasn't been like this for years.

Silence reigns. No star in heaven hears
the subtle, scuttling last retreat of death.
He thinks it hasn't been like this for years;
it would be such an effort to draw breath.

The subtle, scuttling last retreat of death
rolls the stone aside, and now the breeze
suggests the effort of unsteady breath.
Nothing in this life is done with ease.

Stone rolled aside. The movement of the breeze
stirs the acrid dust upon the floor.
Not so, he thinks; the one thing done with ease
is dying. Living always summons more.

Again the acrid dust stirs on the floor.
Another moment: could he just abide
in dying? Living summons. There is more:
they want his blood, their fingers in his side.

Another moment. Rest, and just abide.
But then the nostrils twitch and muscles move;
the blood flows into fingers at his side,
rising from the deep abyss of Love.

The nostrils twitch, and now the muscles move.
Neither earth beneath, nor hell below
can stop this rising river, deep with Love.
His time has come. He slips into the flow.

Antiphon for the Empty Tomb

O Fire!
> **Burn everything we believe, 'til there is only you.**

O Darkness!
> **Enshroud our eyes, that we at last may see.**

O Light!
> **Illumine hearts that, blind, we see the true.**

O Water!
> **Pull us down, that drowning, we are free.**

O Desire!
> **Yearn in us that we may yearn for you.**

O Wisdom!
> **Beginning of all thought, all thought inspire.**

O Understanding!
> **Thought-shaper, bind the chaos in our brains.**

O Love!
> **Set our hope ablaze with holy fire.**

O Judgment!
> **Love's limit, fire by Fire constrained**

O Beauty!
> **Empty, yet not by Emptiness consumed.**

O Perseverance!
> **Death's stony portal on its hinges turn.**

O Majesty!
> **Flesh surrendered, life from life resumed.**

O Foundation!
> **Rise with the dawn; for we have much to learn!**

Prayer: The Exsultet

Rejoice, O heavenly powers! Sing,
O massed angelic choir!
For Jesus Christ our risen King
wears now the crown of briars.
The dark of sin,
he gathers in;
'til morning dawns with brilliant Fire—
the Light to which our souls aspire.

[*A brief sermon may follow.*]

WATER

The Crossing II

*[To be read as the community
gathers at the font.]*

Remember the parting of chaos
deep in the darkness, before the first Fire
falls from the stars, 'ere the first day is
born in the mists of the mind of Desire.

Remember the floods broken free
from primordial rivers above and below,
and the promise-keeled frigate asea;
life atop death, it drifts in the flow

'til bereft of a hope for tomorrow
the raft runs aground on an infinite Love
that bears the first respite from sorrow:
the tree of redemption in the beak of a dove.

Remember the parting of waters,
and the far bank's ascent in the dubious night;
remember the sons and the daughters
who followed the Fire in the flickering Light

and arrived at equivocal stations
still wet from the surging of uncertain tides

and eager to give birth to nations,
still yearning to see what the name of God hides.

Remember the torrent of rainfall
soaking a land that knows aught but thirst
and the silence of gods whose names, called,
have nothing to say and can do but their worst

while thunder and storm rage, and lightning
falls on the altar of ancestral stone
and dances celestial jigs, singing
songs of the spheres to the One Name alone.

Remember the baptismal floss,
the drops from the brow of our fair pioneer,
the blood of ascent to the cross,
the rending of curtain, the cry of his fear

that now, in the ultimate parting,
must open a hole that denies all repair.
Yet here the whole earth's deepest smarting
receives of the salve that will soothe its despair.

Then remember your own true oblation
renewed in the spray of this holiest night,
and rejoice at the great confirmation:
Fire-born, Desire names you Children of Light.

[*The Prayer of Thanksgiving over Water and
the Service of Reaffirmation of Baptism follow.*]

MEAL

The Invitation

*[To be read as the community
gathers at the table.]*

You will meet him at the table,
the One who, emptied of Himself, becomes
the Empty space within the heart of Silence,
where Beauty gathers all the world's deep darkness
even now and fills it with the Light.

You will meet him at the table
who calls to you in midnights of the soul
and bids you follow through divided seas
and cross the holy deserts of the heart;
even now you feel the ancient Fire.

You will meet him at the table,
who reaches out to heal the shattered ones,
the dimming shards, the broken, disillusioned,
world-weary, hope long ago abandoned;
even now you see his wounded hands.

You will meet him at the table,
whom you know by many names, inscribed
across the intersticèd universe

or whispered in the smallest breath of love;
even now your lips dare frame their sound.

You will meet him at the table
whom Love now fractures open on the altar,
whom Judgment now decants upon the earth;
his brokenness is rendered up in Beauty
even now, as you take bread and cup.

You will meet him at the table.
He is the host, and holds this space for you,
you who only lately join the feast
and yet are welcomed into realms of Light.
Even now. See, all things are ready.

[*The Great Prayer, the Institution of the meal,
and the serving of the faithful follow.*]

Prayer after Communion

O send us forth in joy, in song
For you have shown us mirth
and in advance of swelling dawn
cast Light upon the earth.
Let now be fed
all those once dead
who languished long in night's sad dearth.
At last they sing the Light's rebirth!

[*A closing hymn is sung, and all are dismissed
with charge and blessing.*]

Illumining Fire

Melody to be used if prayers are sung as part of the vigil.
All prayers fit the meter of this tune.

Ruminations

Fire

(1 Kings 18:20-39)

Fire is at the heart of things.

Traditional celebrations of the paschal vigil begin with the lighting of a fire. It is lit in the normal way: a fire pit is dug, dry wood laid, kindling gathered and positioned, a match struck and the tinder set alight. In that way it is the same as any other fire; hardly anything new about it. Yet the liturgy of the vigil calls this fire "the new fire," because this fire is started fresh (rather than being lit from some other) and exists for one purpose only: to light the brand that will in turn light the paschal candle, the tall white candle that Christians of various persuasions light in worship each week. Mythically speaking, this "new" fire is a gift from God, and the candle lit from it symbolizes for believers the ongoing gift of new life in Christ resulting from the resurrection. It is lit in worship all year, except on Good Friday, the day of the crucifixion of Jesus. That day and the next, Holy Saturday, worship is in darkness. Then, in the darkness of the hours before Easter dawn, a new fire is started and a new candle is lit. Light illumines the darkness once again.

Fire speaks to us about power from beyond us. Fire does not belong to us. Fire has a way of getting out of hand, burning up everything in sight. A still-lit match, an overturned oil lamp, an unextinguished cigarette—tiny fires each—all carry within themselves great conflagrations. Fire can be put out in one place but pop up somewhere else. Fire can be managed, made to work, but something about it refuses to be controlled.

. . .

That's why the story of Elijah and the contest atop Mt. Carmel in 1 Kings 18 is so intriguing. At the heart of the tale is a Fire that refuses to be controlled. And the Fire is, in some mythic way that only a story can understand, God.

Elijah and four hundred fifty prophets devoted to Baal (pronounced "Bah-all") agree to settle a little theological bet: which of the deities they respectively worship is religiously reliable? Is it the God of Israel's ancestors, who was their companion on the long sojourn through divided sea and holy desert, whose name revealed to Moses is so holy that one dare neither pronounce nor write it? Or is it Baal, strongman of the Canaanite pantheon, a sort of ancient near eastern Apollo who rides atop the storm clouds and brings fertility and fecundity and financial well-being?

Ancient Israel seems to have been given to hedging its theological bets. The ancestral deity may have been an adequate resource for desert semi-nomads, following flocks from well to watering hole, relying on the kindness of others who shared the same nomadic paths. But farms and fields and a food supply dependent on the skies darkening and opening with blessed and predictable rain—all these raise new questions about the old system. Are the old ways up to the challenges of a new day? Why not offer a bull or two to Baal, just to be on the safe side?

But that's the problem with gods: they're all or nothing. Israel's ancestral deity will brook no competition. As the opening salvo in this war in the heavens, Israel's god sends the prophet Elijah (whose name is a little religious truth-claim: "My God is Yah") to invade territory supposedly under the aegis of Baal. In the previous chapter of 1 Kings, Elijah has proclaimed a cessation of the rains—a drought, the sort of thing thought to be controlled by Baal. The gathered corps of four hundred fifty prophets of Baal cannot let this insult stand and set out to prove their god, not Elijah's, is lord. Hence the contest atop the mountain.

The contest is simple, elemental. Two identical altars, two identical bulls slain and slaughtered for sacrifice, two equally fervent communities of faith. All that is missing is Fire. Each side beseeches its divine patron for heavenly Fire, for a lightning bolt to immolate the altar. Each side is sure that its deity will comply.

Perhaps the outcome of this contest is clear before it ever begins. In the days leading up to the contest, Baal seems incapable of overruling the pesky prophet (Elijah's own king calls him "Troubler of Israel") and breaking the grip of drought. Once it is underway, things do not improve for Baal and his prophets. They do their utmost: dancing the sacred limping dance, praying fervent prayers that have always worked in the past, even ritually gashing their flesh to display their devotion. But nothing works. Perhaps Baal is waiting for some still-more-impassioned display on the part of his acolytes. Perhaps he is pre-occupied. Perhaps, as Elijah sarcastically suggests, the deity is cranky and in need of a nap. No matter; there is no fire from Baal.

Then it is Elijah's turn. With a flair for the dramatic, the prophet proceeds to raise the stakes. In a time of drought, he commands that bucket after bucket of precious water be dumped over the altar, drenching the bull and the wood and the stones and running down onto the parched earth—a soggy sacrifice and a scandalous waste. If he is no better than his counterparts at summoning fire, his countrymen will surely bring his ministry to an abrupt and painful end. The prophet prays, but not a prayer of desperation or lament. Rather, he simply asks the ancestral deity to *be* the ancestral deity. And lo, from the heavens, Fire falls.

Fire is at the heart of things.

. . .

Jewish mysticism has long held that, at the beginning of creation, the Infinite—who is everything and nothing and all—allows to fall into creation a bit of the Fire that is the Infinite, a single blinding ray of Light that is the beginning of Things. The Fire is the starting place, the beginning of the beginning of the beginning. Everything else proceeds from the Fire that falls. Even the notion of "God." God is Fire.

. . .

When the Fire falls upon Elijah's altar, it burns up the bull, consumes the wood, cracks the stones, and licks up all the water on the ground. No well-managed sacrifice, this. It is a conflagration, an inferno. It pays no regard to safety. It respects no limit on religious enthusiasm. The Fire is out of control. Beyond control. That's the way it is with Fire. It burns up everything we value and makes us start again.

. . .

In the darkness of Holy Saturday we gather around the fire-pit where there is, as yet, no fire. In the liturgical rhythm of the Christian Holy Week, the crucifixion is behind us. With the death of Jesus, everything his followers have hoped for has been consumed in the all-consuming fire of Roman wrath. The dead body has been lowered from the cross and placed in the tomb, and a stone rolled up to cover the entrance, sealing inside the dreams believers have dared to dream, and leaving on the outside those foolhardy enough to dream them. The tomb is the dead end. Time to give up, pack it in, cash in your chips.

And then there is New Fire.

The gospels don't allow us into the tomb in the dark hours of Holy Saturday, any more than does Genesis allow us behind the curtain drawn across the "before" of creation by Scripture's opening phrase "In the beginning...." But the faithful imagination dares go where logic and sometimes even theology fear to tread. Just as the great traditions of Jewish mysticism speak of the Fire from which springs all life, may not imagination conjure up the vision of the Fire in the darkness from which springs Light and Life? It is the Fire that burns up the past and all its dead ends. The Fire that starts world all over again. The Fire that rolls aside the stone and emerges from the darkness as the first light of a new creation. The Fire is still burning out of control.

Fire is at the heart of things.

'Ein Sof—The Infinite

The readings of the vigil begin at the beginning, with Genesis 1. And Genesis begins: *Bereshith 'Elohim*—"In the beginning, God...."

The first word of Scripture—*bereshith*—is a kind of curtain drawn across the stage of the narrative of the world, hiding everything behind it from view. It is not so much that there is no "before" but that, in the eyes of the writers of Genesis, the "before" is unknowable, inaccessible. *Bereshith* is a barrier placed across the intellectual path of the reader, as if to say, "thus far and no farther." There is a limit to how far back language can convey us. Beyond this edge of the linguistic map, there be dragons.

But what if we imagine a beginning before the beginning? Even if there are limits on language, are there perhaps not such limits on imagination? What can imagination say of what lies behind the curtain, of the "God" before "In the beginning, God...?"

Mysticism imagines a way into the silence before the *bereshith* of Genesis—a way into the darkness before the birth of light, into the time when there was no *before*, into the space where there is no *where*, into a condition in which there is no *thing*. Jewish mystics call that condition *'Ein Sof*. The phrase literally means, "there is no end," but if used as a nominative it can be fairly translated "the Infinite."

It is tempting to assume that "*'Ein Sof*" or "the Infinite" is merely another way of saying "God," and in some ways this is true; we are certainly speaking of something we would call divinity. But in speaking of "God" we dichotomize reality by assuming that, if there is a "God," there is also a "not-God." Such logic cannot be applied to Jewish mystical speculation, for the simple reason that it requires two modes of being—God and not-God—rather than the radical oneness of the Infinite, which is all-in-all.

In speaking of the Infinite, Jewish mystics—and their Neoplatonist forebears before them—contemplate a sole, limitless, monistic reality from and within which nothing can be differentiated. Before the creation of the cosmos and prior to a condition in which there might exist a being called

"God"—indeed, prior to being itself, if such things are imaginable—there "is" "only" ʾ*Ein Sof,* the Infinite.

We tend to throw around the term "infinite" far too casually, as if it describes something merely "really big" or "really long" but doesn't bankrupt our capacities of thought. In fact, "infinite" means having no end. Which also means having no beginning. There is no edge to the reality of the Infinite, nothing that is not the Infinite. There is no time when the Infinite is not, because the reality of the Infinite stands outside of and apart from time itself. The Infinite has no being, because being itself is a thing, and the Infinite is beyond all things. The Infinite is beyond being and non-being.

ʾ*Ein Sof* —the Infinite—is a theological singularity: a unique and unrepeatable condition out of which all other conditions and categories arise, and whose behavior obeys no laws and cannot be described. Categories of time and space and the edges and limitations they imply—and ultimately even being and its antithesis, non-being—cease to have meaning. There "is" "only" the Infinite. Language trips over its own clumsy feet. The mind resists.

Part of the resistance is that we—and here "we" refers at least to all the Western religious traditions—are accustomed to thinking of the divine in personal, even anthropomorphic terms. We objectify God, give "God" a name so that the experience can be identified and perhaps managed. We use pronouns—"he" and "him" in the most limited form but in truth, any pronoun—as a way of abbreviating the Infinite for purposes of description. We employ metaphors like "the hand of God" or "the face of God," none of which can finally have meaning because they contemplate realities that are limited by our objectification of them. In the presence of the Infinite, all this must fall away.

But part of the resistance, in at least the Trinitarian tradition, is that "God" is known and understood in relational terms: Father, Son, and Spirit. The language traditionally used to describe the Trinity—classically "one God in three Persons"—supports the personal, relational character of thought about God. Trinitarian faith holds that this relational character is not merely a metaphor, nor only a characteristic of human interaction with God, but something intrinsically true of the nature of God. The notion of the immanent Trinity—that God actually *is* triune, and the triune nature is not merely a characteristic of the way God appears in and to the world (the "economic Trinity")—seems to resist mysticism's radical singularity of ʾ*Ein Sof*. Are the two at an impasse? Perhaps. Perhaps not. There will be more to say of this.

But whatever else we say, we must begin with the unknowable, irreducible, indivisible, silent reality of ʾ*Ein Sof*. It responds to no inquiry, permits no examination, offers no clues to how it can be what it can be. The Infinite is the opposite of personal and relational; it is universal and impassive. It does not move, is not moved, because it transcends notions of motion and place. It cannot be known because there is no other than the Infinite to know it. It cannot be divided or categorized because there is no mind or will apart from it to measure its dimensions or weigh its mass. It absorbs all questions and offers no answers. This is the death of logic.

But not, it would seem, the death of imagination . . . .

Sefirot—The Ten Names of God

'Ein Sof—the Infinite—is not dormant, at least not in the mystical imagination. Rather, insists the mystical tradition, the Infinite pulses with life. And that life is defined in Jewish mysticism in two ways. The first is the *sefirot*.

Sefirot (singular: *sefirah*) is a Hebrew term meaning something like "emanations." Immediately, there is a problem. To think of something "emanating" from a source is to suggest that the emanation" is produced by, derived from, a source, something that has a separate and dependent relationship to that source . But such is not the case with the *sefirot*. They are *within*, not derived from, the Infinite. They are expressions of the Infinite. They are not merely ways of experiencing the Infinite. They *are* the Infinite. They are in the same relationship as are the Christian notions of the economic and immanent Trinity; as the Infinite expresses itself in the *sefirot*, so the Infinite actually is. In the Jewish mystical tradition, the *sefirot* are often called "the ten names of God."

Classically, the ten *sefirot* are depicted in a vertical configuration sometimes called "the Tree of Life." There is a bewildering variety of such depictions, reaching back seventeen hundred years or more. But in a simplified form, the configuration looks something like this:

The *Sefirot*

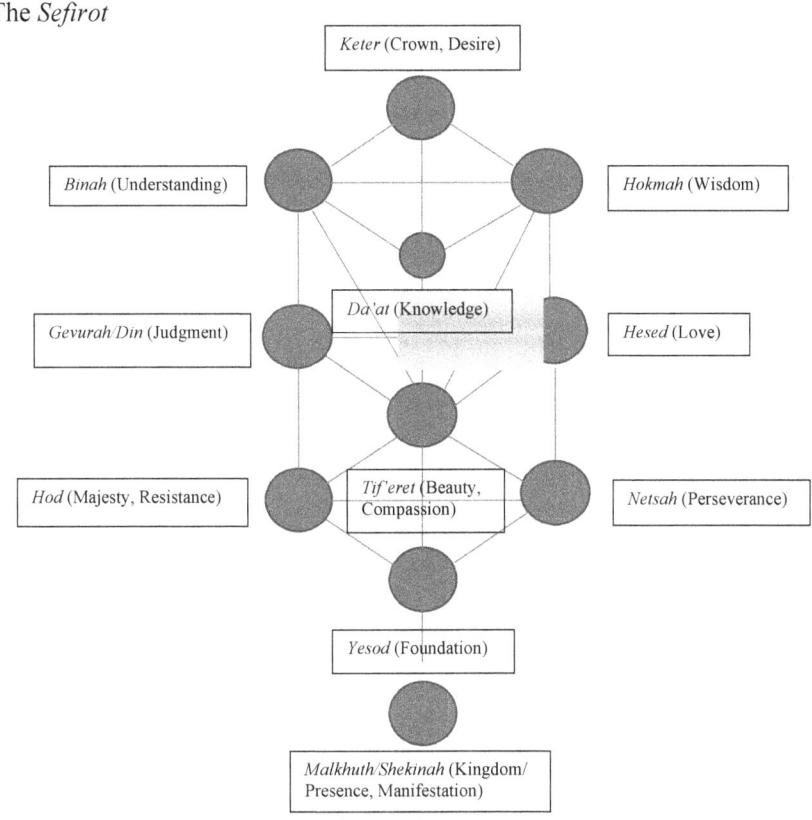

The relationship among the *sefirot* is among the most bewildering elements of Jewish mystical speculation, occupying scholars and mystics in endless permutations of meaning. The present ruminations do not pretend competence in that speculation. But perhaps there are basic observations that will fuel the imagination, a few hesitant steps into realms unknown.

First among the *sefirot* is *Keter* (Crown), thought of as the primordial Will, divine Desire. It is closest to the Infinite, the most essential and basic expression of the identity of the Infinite. *Keter* is the urge to create—formless, unrestrained, undefined, raw. *Keter* is the Infinite yearning toward creation, the most elemental impetus (more about this below).

The energy and essence of the Infinite expressed in *Keter* is channeled through *Ḥokmah* (Wisdom) and *Binah* (Understanding), in the way perhaps that all creative desire must be filtered through the tension between blinding flashes of insight and disciplined understanding. *Ḥokmah* and

Binah together form *Daʿat* (Knowledge). *Daʿat* is not thought of as one of the *sefirot*, but as an interior aspect of the Infinite, a by-product of the process of its self-expression. Knowledge is the integration of Wisdom and Understanding that gives direct expression to Desire. The two, *Ḥokmah* and *Binah*, initiate an oppositional structure in the *sefirot*—the "right" and "left" sides. Aspects of the Infinite stand in tension with one another, with energies generally positively and generously disposed on the "right" side and those characterized by sternness, limitation, or judgment on the "left." These three *sefirot* are also called the "higher" *sefirot* and are thought of as closest to the reality of the Infinite.

The oppositional pattern continues with the "lower" *sefirot*, beginning with *Ḥesed* (Love, Kindness) and *Gevurah* (sometimes called *Din*; Discipline, Judgment). The energies of the Infinite, passing through these *sefirot*, are expressed in *Tifʾeret* (Beauty, Compassion), sometimes called the "bolt" to hold the Tree together, serving as its unifying element. *Tifʾeret* locates Beauty in the very being of the divine, not as a thing perceived by an observer, but as an aspect central to the identity of the Infinite, an expression of its essential nature. *Tifʾeret* is also directly connected to *Keter* through *Daʿat*—Beauty connected to Desire through Knowledge—hinting at an invitation offered by Beauty to seek after knowledge of the deepest nature of the divine.

Netsaḥ (Perseverance) and *Hod* (Majesty, Resistance) again reflect the pairing of *sefirot*, introducing a balancing tension between the impulse to press ever toward self-expression in creation and a refusal to surrender the prerogative of divine glory. *Netsaḥ* is the persistence of the divine movement toward creation; *Hod* is the refusal to accept that which does not reflect the divine majesty and glory in that creation. *Netsaḥ* is the force that presses back the waters of the sea to allow Israel through; *Hod* is the release of those waters, so that they return to the way God created them to flow. *Netsaḥ* is "I will be your God and you will be my people"; *Hod* is "you shall have no other gods before me."

Yesod (Foundation) is the *sefirah* of collection and gathering, where the creative energies of the eight *sefirot* above it are focused and readied to impregnate creation. *Yesod* is often imagined as the divine male genitalia, essential in creativity and generativity. *Yesod* is the wholeness of the principles by which creation works, the "unified field theory" that guides both atoms and galaxies. *Yesod* is the gathering place of the stories that will form the sacred history, the commandments and narratives that will give identity to those whom God calls. *Yesod*, perhaps, is the reservoir of all the sacred words that constitute the story of God. Dare one say that *Yesod* is Logos, the Word that underlies all that is?

And *Malkhuth* (Kingdom, Manifestation) is ʾ*Ein Sof* complete in self-expression, knowable in creation and history. *Malkhuth* is often called *Shekinah*, the presence of God in and through the created world. *Malkhuth/Shekinah* is the womb in which the being of God is birthed in the world, the feminine principle to *Yesod's* masculinity. Such language inevitably evokes Christian thoughts of Mary, the mother of Jesus, the "god-bearer," and in much Catholic piety the feminine principle of the divine. *Malkhuth* gives birth to what begins in *Keter*, the manifestation of divine desire expressed through Wisdom and Understanding, moved by Love and disciplined by Judgment, pressed ever ahead by Perseverance and challenged by Resistance, gathered in story and law and hope. *Malkhuth* is God among us, the Infinite in our midst. Dare one say, "Immanuel?"

Mysticism in both Christian and Jewish traditions has imagined that the energies of the Infinite do not flow in only one direction, but pulse back and forth, "up" and "down" between the Infinite and the world. There is a constant inhaling and exhaling, if such metaphors can be employed, that is ever drawing in and pushing out, gathering and scattering the energies of the Infinite. So too with creation: God creates and calls into being, and all beings seek return to their Creator.

To go back to where we began, recall that the generation of the *sefirot* is a process *within* the Infinite. Think of the *sefirot* perhaps as a metaphor for the unknowable nature of the Infinite, a schematic diagram of the ineffable. Think of them as the "ten names" the Infinite bestows upon itself. Think of them as the Infinite yearning in the direction of creation. Creation, whether of the universe or of any of its parts or participants, is first and finally a process *within the Infinite*, before it is ever apart from the Infinite. Creation is whole within God, before it is ever particular within its own time and place. The true home, the source for all that is and all we are, is the being of the Infinite. Creation cannot survive without its Creator, moving, pulsing, ebbing and flowing in and through it. The finite cannot be without the Infinite.

Light and Desire

And the second way Jewish mysticism expresses the life of *'Ein Sof*? It begins with Light.

Back to the beginning. Genesis 1:3: God says, "Let there be light." The command illumines the primordial darkness and makes the first division of creation possible: light is separated from darkness, day from night. In all the eons since, believers of various traditions have emphasized the dichotomy. Light opposes darkness, and darkness light. Light is safe, good, beautiful; darkness is malevolent, fearsome, full of threat.

But imagination dares suggest that things are not as they seem.

Physicists say that light—that is to say, visible light—is a form of electromagnetic radiation occupying a relatively narrow band width (400-700 nanometers, if one can conceive of such infinitesimal distances) of the spectrum of such radiation known in the physical universe. Visible light travels in waves. But the curious thing about light is that, when a body absorbs it, it is absorbed in the same way that particles of matter are absorbed, and that at the moment of absorption the wave collapses, leading to the oddity that light is both wave and particle, both motion and thing in motion.

Light is not one thing or another, but both and neither.

...

One of challenges posed by mysticism is escaping the mindset that the essence of a thing is only one thing, and not multiple things, even multiple contradictory things. Physics says that light is both particle and wave, and neither particle only nor wave only. Might imagination suggest that light is both light and dark? In the singularity of the Infinite, before the dawn of creation, does the duality of light and dark collapse into a single reality that is not one or the other, but both and neither?

One might wonder about such thoughts because of the limitations of our language. We have no experience of either light or dark that does not involve the other. We experience light not in the absolute but as the absence or diminution of darkness. We experience darkness as the absence or diminution of light. To speak of the one is to speak of the other. The perception of either light or darkness is conditioned on the perception of its opposite.

But before *bereshith,* the beginning, in the undivided unity that is the Infinite, there are no opposites, no distinctions, no separation. There is only the Infinite, in whom light and dark are one thing, and nothing, and everything, because they are the Infinite. Before the first command, there is both light and dark, and neither light nor dark, because the duality of light over against darkness does not exist.

Why does the Infinite move from the perfect serenity of absolute unity to the multitudinous cacophony of oppositional reality? Why does God command the being of light? The questions beckon us into the life of the Infinite, and especially into Desire.

Highest and first among the *sefirot* is *Keter,* (Crown). The energy of *Keter* is that of the Will, Desire—undisciplined, untrammeled yearning. That *Keter*—Desire—is the highest and first of the sefirot is a way of affirming that the essence of the Infinite is alive, seeking some way of self-expression. Keter is Desire expressed in its purest form, before it has been illumined with the insight of Ḥokmah (Wisdom) or structured by *Binah* (Understanding). As the mystics imagine it, *Keter* is the most basic, most elemental, most authentic expression of the divine, the "name" of God, the closest to the heart of God. *Keter* is the Infinite as Desire.

But desire for what? In the absolute unity of the Infinite, there is nothing that lies outside the Infinite to be desired. How can there be Desire if there is no object of desire?

Imagine that Desire and the object of Desire are one, as dark and light are one—as indeed the whole of creation, with all its bewildering variety, is one—in the singularity of ʾ*Ein Sof.* Imagine that, within the Infinite, Desire is all, and all is Desire, because the Infinite is Desire. Imagine that Desire is the essence of the Infinite, the Infinite yearning toward creation.

Christian theology long ago postulated that the nature of God is Love, a love so pure, so deep, so powerful, that it overflows itself and creates within itself the Beloved. If such can be said, then perhaps it is also to be said that there is within God both Beloved and the One Who Loves. But this effulgence of Love is not a binary and static reality. Between the Lover and the Beloved, moving back and forth, is Love Itself, coursing from Lover to Beloved, each making the other both Lover and Beloved, Desirer and

Desired. The triune God, says Christian theology, is Desirer, Desired, and Desire, perfect Love, complete in itself. And yet . . . .

. . . not dormant in its perfection. For the Love, the Desire that is God, overflows yet more, spilling over into the darkness and emptiness of the "before." Love, the Desire of God, is the expression of God in every aspect of creation, pulsing in the veins and surging in the waves and flowing like a silent river through the aquifers beneath the basement of the world. All that is, all that will be, is the expression of Love, finds the source of its life in the Love, the Desire that is God. And because it is born of Desire, the world of Desire returns Desire to the Desirer. The Love, the Desire of God, is at the heart of everything there is.

. . .

The Gospel of John begins with this:

> In the beginning was the Word, and the Word was with God, and the Word was God. He was in the beginning with God. All things came into being through him, and without him not one thing came into being. What has come into being in him was life, and the life was the light of all people. The light shines in the darkness, and the darkness did not overcome it (John 1:1-5).

The Greek term we translate "word" is, of course, *Logos*, a term that underlies "logic" and every form of "-ology" known to the human mind. But "word"—even capitalized—is too small a term for the vast expanse of *Logos*. For that matter, any of the other broad range of translational possibilities—matter, thing, principle, idea, etc.—suffers the same limitation. "Expression" might get closer, if we do not limit the medium of expression to speech or writing or any of the other ways in which we use words. Expression, in the sense that something of the essence of God inevitably, ineluctably, eternally, and constantly moves outward from itself, makes itself accessible, intelligible, perceivable, available. Expression, as in Desire expressing itself in and through the world. Expression, as in the Desirer and the Desired expressing their Desire in and through the being of the world.

And that Expression expresses itself in the command: "Let there be Light."

. . .

Jewish mysticism imagines that, before the *bereshith,* as Desire wells in the Infinite, it overflows in a single ray of Light, thinner than a hair, brighter than all the brilliance of all the suns and stars that are yet to be. Light falls from the "crown"—*Keter*—of the Infinite. It is the Light that creates the *sefirot.* It is the Light that becomes the light of suns and the stars. It is, as John will have it, "the Light of the World." This Light that is Expression, that is Love, that is Desire, is with God. The Light is God. Creator and creation. And without the Light, nothing that is made comes into being. The Light creates the darkness, and in the darkness we know the Light. And long as Light and dark have struggled one against the other, the one has not overcome the other, because the one cannot exist without the other.

Light is Desire is the Infinite, overflowing into itself and ultimately beyond itself. Light is Desire is the Infinite illumining itself and ultimately all that is not itself. Light is Desire is the Infinite, making itself and making all that will come to be.

Tzimtzum—The Hole in the Heart of God

"And God said, 'let there be . . .'" So Genesis says.

One might be forgiven for assuming that the first act of creation is God speaking a word into the void, a word that calls creation into being. But what if the first act of creation is not God exhaling breath in speech, but inhaling breath in preparation to speak? What if the beginning of the beginning is not God moving outward in sound but drawing inward in silence? What if the beginning of creation is not the making of a world, but the making of an emptiness in which there is the possibility of a world? What if there is a hole in the heart of God?

. . .

Jewish mysticism in the sixteenth century produced a great school of mythic imagination in the town of Safed, in the Galilee, in what was at the time Ottoman Syria. Perhaps foremost among its scholars was Isaac Luria, whose name is now wedded to mystical speculation throughout Judaism and beyond. Luria received from the millennia before him the notions of *'Ein Sof*, the Infinite, and the *sefirot*, the "ten names." He understood *Keter* as the Desire of the Infinite, straining toward self-expression in creation. But he also inherited a problem, one faced by Neoplatonist scholars from the second century CE onward: if the Infinite is all-in-all, and there "is" "nothing" "other" than the Infinite and no place other than the Infinite for any other thing to be—how then can there come into being anything that is not the Infinite? If the Infinite is the all-encompassing, undifferentiated unity, how can "being" exist, particularly if "being" must be distinguished from "non-being"? For Luria, the question was this: where and into what shall the effulgence of Desire overflow if the Infinite is everything and everywhere?

What if, Luria asked, the first act of creation was not the Infinite *overflowing* into the *sefirot*, God moving outward from the serenity of absolute unity, but the Infinite *withdrawing*, contracting itself into itself, making within God a space that is not-God? Luria called this withdrawal *tzimtzum*, a term he borrowed from the Talmud. There, *tzimtzum* refers to

God concentrating the divine presence—the *Shekinah*—into a single point within the Holy of Holies in the Temple. Luria reversed the direction of movement. Instead of concentrating the Infinite, Luria imagined that the Infinite makes an emptiness, a space no larger than a single point, within the Infinite. That one single point is infinitely small, but it is the space within which all that is not-God—all creation, either mystical or physical—comes into being. *Tzimtzum* is the hole in the heart of God.

Such important imaginings spring from this insight! If the first act of creation is not effulgence but evacuation, not a flowing of Desire but an ebbing of it, then one can say that Desire is restrained, limited, structured by *tzimtzum*.

And perhaps one can see in that structuring of Desire the first inklings of the triadic function of the uppermost three *sefirot*: *Keter* (Desire), raw and unrestrained, is given the insight and direction toward creation in *Ḥokmah* (Wisdom) and at the same time restrained, shaped, limited by *Binah* (Understanding). No longer raw and unrestrained, the creative impulse of the Infinite is beginning to take shape and substance. Structure and form are part of the essence of the Infinite, because they make Desire creative.

If the first act of creation is the creation not of something but of nothing, not of a thing but of a void in which a thing might come to be, then can one say that being arises from nothingness? Creation, according to most Christian theology, is *ex nihilo*, out of nothing. God creates a world not from some pre-existing matter or energy, but exactly in the absence of matter and energy, in the one place where nothing truly exists. *Tzimtzum* leads one to imagine that before *tzimtzum*, there is neither something nor nothing, and both something and nothing, because the potential for both something and nothing are inherent in the limitless possibilities of the Infinite. But with the creation of nothing, there is also created the possibility of something, and thus the distinction between something and nothing is born.

If the first act of creation is the creation of distinction—between something and nothing—then can one say that the first distinction is God and not-God? Before *tzimtzum*, the potential of both God and not-God exists in the limitless possibilities of the Infinite. But in *tzimtzum*, one imagines that the Infinite ceases to be infinite, accepting limitation in the existence of a place that is not the Infinite. If the Infinite ceases to be infinite, it is no longer *'Ein Sof*, "without end." The birthing of not-God is also the birth of God. It is the hole in the heart of God that makes God God.

Is the *tzimtzum* literal or metaphorical? Should Luria's myth be regarded as an account of what happened or a poetic way of explaining what is? Scholars of Jewish mysticism have argued this question for centuries. But . . . does it matter? In a theology borne aloft by imagination, "how did it happen?" seems less important than "what do we learn?". Like the story of Adam and Eve in the Garden, the power of the narrative is in the telling, not in the factuality of the thing told.

But this much can be said: there is something deeply fascinating about the idea that the first act of creation is not the creation of something, but the creation of nothing. Not the making of a world to fill a void, but the making of a void to be filled by a world. That the very first act of a God whom we have come to know as "Love" is not to come closer in intimacy, but to withdraw into self-isolation and alienation. Indeed, perhaps most fascinating of all is the ironic realization that love is expressed first not in divine intimacy, but in divine abandonment.

. . .

God, it seems, has a record of abandonment in crucial moments; such a God has even acquired a theological title: *Deus absconditus*, the God who absconds. Jesus on the cross, in the moment of highest agony, cries out in Aramaic, *'Eloi,'Eloi, lema' sabacthani*, "My God, my God, why have you abandoned me?" (Mark 15:34). In the moments before the darkness of death closes over him, Christ experiences *tzimtzum*, the withdrawal of God. Christian theology understands the nature of God the Creator and God the Christ to be one, but in this moment of supreme pain they are suddenly and excruciatingly divided. There will be more to say of this.

For now, it is worth recalling that *tzimtzum* is the prelude to the possibility of creation, the Infinite *inhaling* itself into itself before exhaling the first commandment into creation. One imagines the cross as the theater of *tzimtzum*. God inhales, withdraws. The curtain tears in the Holy of Holies. The stone is rolled against the door of the tomb. Inside, there is an empty space, an infinite darkness. Outside, the whole world waits for a new creation. It is as though the tomb is the womb from which that new creation is born. Metaphors abound. But make no mistake: here at the world's ragged edge, in the darkness of Golgotha, the beginning of the new creation is an act of withdrawal, a *tzimtzum*. A hole in the heart of God.

Love and Judgment

The paschal vigil readings usually contain the recitation of the ʿ*Akedah*, the story of the "binding" of Isaac in Genesis 22. To read this tale is to be bathed in the cold sweat of terror, unsettled by dark visions of a God who requires human sacrifice. And not just any human sacrifice will do, but the sacrifice of the one upon whom rests every hope for the future that God has promised. It is a story that exchanges life for death, hope for fear, possibilities for dead ends.

Imagination suggests that the command comes in the wee hours of night. "Take your son, your *only* son," commands the God of darkness, and as if to twist the knife, adds " . . . *whom you love* . . . ." Sacrifices—ʿ*oloth*, "whole burnt offerings," in the language of the Law—are called for and agreed to, arrangements made, and "early in the morning" Abraham and Isaac set out, accompanied by two of Abraham's servants, on the three day's journey to Mt. Moriah.

Three days of silence follow, during which the imagination rages with emotion: fear, confusion, dark determination, anxiety, and exhaustion all mingle in a noxious psychic soup. But no one speaks. Not a word is spoken until on the third day Abraham dismisses the servants and loads the wood onto the shoulders of Isaac. Only then does Isaac break the silence to ask the question so terrible in its innocence: "Father . . . the fire and the wood are here, but where is the lamb?" We know the answer. But we have questions of our own. What sort of father loves a son and kills him? What sort of God would command such a thing? What sort of Love obeys such a command? What sort of Law would require it?

. . .

In the mystical logic of the *sefirot*, Ḥ*esed* (Love) appears on the "right" side of the Tree of Life, where *sefirot* characterized as generous and expansive are positioned. Its partner, *Gevurah* (Resistance), often named *Din* (Judgment), appears on the "left", the restrictive, demanding, rigorous side.

Like *Ḥokmah* and *Binah* above them, they subject the creative energies of *Keter* to a kind of tempering process, annealing those energies into something new, in the way a strip of metal is tempered and annealed into a knife blade. *Ḥesed* (Love) is Desire expressed as steadfast love, the sense of mutuality and connection that lies at the heart of every strong, enduring relationship, whether a marriage or the faithfulness of God in covenant with Israel. It gives itself in self-sacrificing altruism; it yearns for the well-being of the other, even at the cost of its own. It is what the Greeks called *agape*, the love of God for humankind, and the love that binds together the true fellowship of the faithful.

Over against *Ḥesed* stands *Gevurah/Din*, heat-stressing Love with Judgment, tempering self-giving with covenantal expectation of obedience. One of the oldest texts of Jewish mysticism, the *Bahir*, says this of *Gevurah*:

> It is that regarding which it is written, "And fire came down and consumed the burnt offering, and the stones, and the earth, and evaporated the water that was in the trench" (1 Kings 18:38) It is also written, "The Lord your God is a consuming fire, a jealous God (Deuteronomy 4:24). (*Bahir*, saying no. 135).

Gevurah is the Fire that burns up everything and from which everything must start anew.

The *sefirot* have occasionally been identified with biblical characters whose stories seemed to suggest similarities with the character of a given *sefirah*. Abraham is identified with *Ḥesed* because he is understood to possess an abundant love that will include a whole nation, a love wholly devoted and obedient to God. Even when that God demands his entire future as an assay of that devotion, Abraham does not hesitate. Isaac, by contrast, is seen as characterizing *Gevurah/Din*, strict justice and adherence to law, perhaps because Isaac makes not a whimper of protest, offers not a whiff of reluctance to obey. He appears simply to accept as a matter of course that the sacrifice required by a dark, bizarre divine justice is the blood that courses through his own veins.

...

The Christian Passion story tells us that, on the night of his arrest, after Jesus and his disciples had shared the Passover, they went to Gethsemane, a sort of public garden in Jerusalem, where Jesus began to pray. "Father, if you are willing, remove this cup from me; yet not my will but yours be done"

(Luke 22:42). Three times Jesus prays the prayer, and with such effort that, as Luke has it, "his sweat became like great drops of blood falling down on the ground" (Luke 22:44). But there is no answer. The Father, it seems, has turned a deaf ear. Or, perhaps, cannot bear to speak the only answer there is. Instead, there is silence in the garden, save for the snoring of the disciples. The silence is unbroken until the temple guards come to arrest Jesus and take him away for trial, and the story moves on toward its end on the cross. Not all prayers have answers. Not all answers are those prayed for.

. . .

Dark stories raise dark questions. What sort of Father kills his own Son? What sort of justice requires the spilling of blood? What sort of God stands by in silence while the deed is done? How long will the spilling of blood— on ancient mountains and in Jerusalem gardens and on skull-shaped promontories and in the gutters of a thousand city streets—be deemed the price that Love must pay to live in the world?

. . .

Ḥesed and Gevurah/Din, Love and Judgment, eternally strain against each other in the configuration of the *sefirot*. Their friction heats and hones the movement of Desire, shaping the being of God and whetting the will to create. The result is *Tif'eret* (Beauty). *Tif'eret* is equal parts Love and Judgment and is the mixture of Love and Judgment that creation can tolerate. Pure Love is boundless, rich, overflowing, overflowing the creation Love creates. Pure Judgment is harsh and unyielding, restrictive and vindictive, cutting away the very excesses Love generates. Creation trembles with the fullness of a Love it cannot contain. Creation quakes with the fear of a Judgment held like a blade to its throat. But in the mixture of the two there is hope. There is possibility. There is Beauty.

    Beauty is not merely a reaction in the mind of the beholder to a sensation. Long before it reaches our senses, Beauty is at the heart of the being of God, the expression of the Infinite pulsing through the being of God. Beauty is God, balanced without faltering or wavering, unerring and unfailing, between Love and Judgment. To know such Beauty is to know God. To know God is to know Beauty.

...

Some say the Christ was born to die. The cross was the inevitable and foreordained end of a life of pure obedience, pure compassion, pure Love. The world cannot contain such Love, it is said, and so Judgment must try and condemn it, mock and deride it, and finally take its life.

Some say the Christ chose to die. The cross, it is said, is the ultimate expression of a Love so pure that Judgment cannot diminish it, derision cannot devalue it, death cannot defeat it. It lays down its life.

Some say the Christ dies to pay a debt. The ledger of weal and woe, long unbalanced through deficit of weal and surfeit of woe, must be set to rights, and only the currency of blood will do. Love hands over its life to Judgment, and the transaction between God and world is done.

I say the Christ dies eternally, is ever and always dying, that he dies in every finite day and place. He dies because Love and Judgment are fired and fused into one, honing divine Desire until it is Beautiful. He dies to create a God whose Beauty illumines every sunrise and sunset, and shines in the stars at night. He dies to create a creation that might receive such Beauty if only it knew where to look.

...

On top of Mt. Moriah, the altar is built of stones as ancient as time, the wood is cut and laid to catch fire, and Isaac is bound hand and foot, prepared as a lamb for the slaughter. The moment has come. Love raises the knife, the agent of Judgment, and now at last the two are become one. The morning sun peeks over the horizon, and its first ray falls like a fiery shaft upon the mountaintop, the altar, the wood, and the man. It falls upon the knife blade, burnished for its task. And the gleam from the blade reflects Light into every corner of creation, a Light so bright all creation is made beautiful in the shining.

Divided Seas

There are moments when all the past comes to a point in the present, and a single decision pivots the whole world toward the future.

. . .

Paschal vigils include the reading of Exodus 14, the dramatic story of Israel's crossing the Red Sea in its escape from slavery in Egypt. It is a tale about Moses and his brother Aaron, and their efforts to persuade Pharaoh to let Israel go from its bondage to worship God on the holy mountain, Sinai. It is a tale of divine Perseverance. It is a tale about passing through waters.

The story is ancient, constitutive. Israel, Abraham's descendants, has lingered in bondage in Egypt for, the text tells us, four hundred thirty years. In all that time, they have come to know what it means to be enslaved, what every people subjected to slavery knows, deep inside their DNA, sometimes long after their slavery ends: they are trapped by a system that takes their labor and gives them nothing in return, a system from which there is no escape. A system that uses them until they are all used up, and then tosses them on the dung heap of time. Nothing in the past gives them reason to believe that the future will ever be any different.

But on this night, someone will make a decision, and everything will change.

The chapters prior to Exodus 14 relate the story of Moses and his brother Aaron as they seek to free Israel from Pharaoh's grasp. They plead, and then they threaten, but Pharaoh is unmoved. The pair then begin calling down plagues on Egypt: a river of blood, frogs, gnats, festering boils, withering hailstorms, locusts. But these, too, fail to convince Pharaoh to relinquish his grip. At last it comes down to the final ace up the divine sleeve. In the midnight darkness, the angel of death passes over the land of Egypt, and anyone whose doorpost is not marked with lamb's blood finds their firstborn child dead. From Pharaoh's palace to the lowest Egyptian hovel, from the shores of the Mediterranean to the edges of the Sahara, the wails of mourning rise like a fog of pain.

Except, of course, from the houses of the Israelites; they are spared. The Israelites have followed Moses' careful instructions to gather their families at table, slaughter and prepare an unblemished lamb, together with bitter herbs, and eat their last enslaved meal standing with shod feet and walking sticks in hand. They have smeared blood on lintel and doorpost to ward off the dark-winged one. They are ready to go. And now, with his land in agony, Pharaoh relents, and Israel takes its leave.

The text doesn't say much about the journey; only that "the Lord went in front of them in a pillar of cloud by day, to lead them along the way, and in a pillar of Fire by night, to give them light."

Such strange symbols for a God to choose! What does one make of such a god? How can one trust such a god? The gods of the world have always chosen concrete things to represent them: bulls, hawks, lions, serpents. The gods of the world have specific homes, sacred places where temples house the presence of the divine. But the god who would be God of Israel chooses the ephemeral, the uncontained, the uncontrolled and uncontrollable. The God of Israel is smoke and Fire, has no home, is always on the move.

Israel get as far as the shores of the Red Sea. There they learn that Pharaoh has changed his mind and dispatched his cavalry to track them down and round them up, and perhaps inflict upon Israel some recompense for Egypt's loss. Before them lie the crystal blue waters of the sea; behind them the swords and spears and pounding hooves of Pharaoh's wrath. Death at either hand. Not for the last time do they wonder why they trust their messiahs, who lead them with bright promises to the dark crossroads of despair. Not for the last time do they wish they had closed their ears, their eyes, their doors to Moses, and gone about their business eking out what living they could fashion in the brickyards of Egypt. The devil you know . . . .

. . . is not always better than the devil you don't. Moses stretches out his hand over the water's edge, and the sea draws up as though it had been insulted, draws up like a massive tsunami withdrawing into the deep before it surges back and obliterates everything in its path. Except that the sea doesn't surge back. Instead it remains withheld, suspended in time and space. Ahead, there stretches a way where before there had only been waves. A way, that is, if you can trust waters that don't behave like waters, and a God who promises deliverance if Israel will but put aside its doubts and follow the pillar of Fire. But can they trust?

Someone must have decided to trust. Someone must have decided that following the Fire was a risk worth taking, even though it offered nothing they didn't already have, and demanded everything they would ever receive. Someone must have done the mental calculation and concluded that the uncertainties of the future were more promising than the certainties of the past. Someone must have been the first to set foot in the mud where a moment before there had been water, to trust that the water would hold long enough to make the crossing. Someone must have been the first, and everyone else followed.

All night the Israelites pass through the divided sea. And when the last of them struggles up the far bank to freedom, mud from the ancient sea bottom still clinging to their sandals, they look back to see the waters closing behind them, swallowing up Pharaoh's chariotry until their shields and spears and horseless harnesses float free and find their way to shore. Free at last, perhaps someone says.

. . .

Why tell this tale on the night while we await the dawn of resurrection? Because the people of God are still passing through waters, following the path through the divided sea. Because this night is a night of decisions, and things will change.

In the ancient practice of the Christian Church, and in many churches even today, the paschal vigil is the night on which those who are new to the faith make a profession of their faith in Christ and come to the water to be baptized. Their baptism is a passing through waters. They go down into the pool or river or kneel before a baptismal font. The promise of baptism is life that no Pharaoh can reach or revoke. An escape from the grip of slavery to sin and the soul's flight to freedom in Christ. The water, the one-to-be-baptized is told, washes away the past and clears a pathway to the future. The water marks the beginning of a new life of faith. The water binds together those who pass through it as a people on their way to meet God.

. . .

Beneath *Ḥesed* and *Gevurah/Din* in the mystical structure of the *sefirot* are *Netsaḥ* and *Hod*. *Netsaḥ* is Perseverance, the sort of doggedness that never surrenders its intended aim, never abandons its quest for the goal. *Netsaḥ* is

God insisting that Pharaoh's "no" will not gainsay the divine command, "Let my people go." *Netsaḥ* is the word that comes again and again to Moses and Aaron on the morning after each plague has resulted in "hardening" Pharaoh's heart: "Rise early and present yourselves to Pharaoh." *Netsaḥ* is the fire in the belly, the longing in the heart, the protest in the street, the vision of the better way. *Netsaḥ* is the idea that there is something other than slavery, than oppression, than death. It is the passionate grip holding to that idea against all odds. *Netsaḥ* is the God who refuses to let go.

Jewish mystics have thought of Moses as the embodiment of *Netsaḥ* for his insistent badgering of Pharaoh with plague and pleading. Moses is God refusing to let go, unwilling to leave Israel in its indolence, undeterred by all its complaining, committed to bringing Israel through the waters to freedom. Moses is God holding back the water, pointing the way through the divided sea until every Israelite has made the crossing. *Netsaḥ* is "I am the Lord your God."

. . .

There are moments when all the past comes to a point in the present, and a single decision pivots the whole world toward the future.

Someone decides to pass through the baptismal waters. Whether it is the individual testing her own new faith, or the parents claiming that faith and all its yet-to-be-fulfilled promises for their as-yet-too-young-to-decide children, someone stands before the waters and considers the risk-benefit ratio of believing. Someone decides to pass through the waters on the way to becoming the people of God.

What is it like to stand at the edge of the baptismal water and say what you believe, without knowing where it will take you or whether it is true? Where does the courage come from to trust that the morning will bring new life, when death still holds the night in its grip? What is it like to decide to follow a god who surrounds you with death in the darkness, even as you are promised forgiveness and freedom? How do you follow a god who withdraws into divine mystery while demanding that you risk everything? How does it feel to step into the water, not knowing whether or when or how you will come out on the other side?

How does it feel to pass through the water, knowing that on every side the waves that might rightfully destroy you are held back in mercy? What wonders are born in your mind as you feel the water close over you, submerging and buoying you, bringing you down to death and making you more alive than you have ever been? What can you do but trust that the same hands that hold back the waves will raise you up from beneath them?

Perseverance is the God who does not allow the waters of the sea to fall back into place until Israel has passed through. Perseverance is the Fire that shines in the darkness to light the way. Perseverance is the hand holding you while the waters close over you and death seems close at hand. Perseverance is the God who refuses to let go.

Holy Deserts, Holy Mountains

> "When Pharaoh let the people go, God did not lead them by way of the land of the Philistines, although that was nearer . . . . So God led the people by the roundabout way of the wilderness" (Ex. 13:17–18).

The Hebrew conjunction we translate "although" in this verse is *ki*, which can, and arguably more often does, translate "because" in English. So we read: "God does not lead them by way of the land of the Philistines *because* it was nearer . . . ." To have gone "by way of the land" would have gotten Israel to Canaan sooner. It would also have been easier, since it would have followed well-established trade routes and gone through communities where food was plentiful. But nothing is easy with God. Israel's God, it seems, is the God of the hard way. The way to God passes through the divided sea and follows the "roundabout way of the wilderness." As Belden Lane observes in his book, *The Solace of Fierce Landscapes*, "Perhaps others can go around the desert on the simpler route toward home, but the way of God's people is always through it."[1]

The stories tell us that, once they climb the sea's far bank, Israel ventures into the desert of Sinai, following the Cloud and the Fire. Day after day, night after night, the Cloud and Fire press on, and the people do what they can to keep up. Water, food, rest, hope—everything is in short supply with no promise of resupply. Who can blame them for complaining—the stories call it "murmuring"—against Moses and Aaron and their mysterious God? This is what you get, perhaps someone says, for following messiahs. No matter. On and on press the Cloud and Fire, and on and on the people stagger.

The goal is Mt. Sinai, probably Jebel Musa in modern geographical terms. A barren peak in the southern tip of the Sinai peninsula, it is physically unimpressive. It is by no means the highest peak in the area; several are significantly loftier. Water is in short supply there; it is hot and dry in

---

1. Belden C. Lane, *The Solace of Fierce Landscapes: Exploring Desert and Mountain Spirituality*. New York: Oxford University Press, 1998, p. 44.

summer, and cold and windswept in winter. Even now, no one lives there, save the occasional penitent who climbs 3,750 steps to the chapel near the summit. The only one to be found there is God.

...

Deserts and mountains.

The classical definitions of a desert—and there are several—mostly center around moisture and rainfall and viability. A place that receives less than an average of 10 inches of rainfall in a year is usually thought of as a desert. A place that cannot sustain vegetation that would, in turn, sustain life. Hunger and thirst, elemental threats to the viability of human life, are the basic characteristics of a desert.

No one survives long in the desert without the systems of support that make human life possible. It is said that the wind and heat in the Sahara will cause the human body to lose a quart of fluid in an hour. If it is true that the average human body contains about 14 gallons of water, it will take slightly less than two and a half days of exposure to the desert wind to render a body a living mummy—and not living for long. Temperature records from the world's deserts compete with one another: air temperatures have been recorded as high as 134° in Death Valley, 136° in Libya; ground temperatures are often considerably higher. The human body can tolerate long term exposure to air temperatures up to around 160° before heat exhaustion occurs, its organs cease to function, and death ensues.

The classical definition of a mountain is a landform that rises prominently above its surroundings, usually at least 300 meters, with slopes that can range from between 10° and 30° in elevation (some are, of course, much higher and steeper). Older ranges support agriculture of various types, but younger, steeper slopes are often barren, windswept, and subject to radical changes in weather patterns and temperatures. Shrouded in clouds and mist, they are places of mystery and challenge. The higher one climbs, the thinner the air and the harder to breathe. Climbers of the world's highest peaks routinely use bottled oxygen to sustain the final phases of their climbs. At the tops of the world's tallest mountains there may literally not be enough air to breathe. Climbers wear clothing suited to polar climates, even though the mountains they climb are often located in equatorial regions.

Why does God deliver the people from slavery, divide the sea to make a way for their escape, only to bring them into the desert to die or, if they live long enough, array them at the foot of a mountain where nothing and no one lives?

...

In the mystical configuration of the *sefirot*, over against *Netsaḥ* is *Hod*. *Hod* is Majesty, and often, Resistance. *Hod* is the demand that accompanies grace, the "no" that is the other side of "yes." *Hod* is the refusal to accept anything less than a people devoted to the pursuit of this *deus absconditus*, willing to suffer thirst and privation and blistered feet on the trek though the holy deserts. *Hod* is the incessant summons to Israel to gather at Mt. Sinai, there to receive the law that will constitute their relationship with this god. If *Netsaḥ* is "I am the Lord your God . . . " a promise uttered beside the water, *Hod* is " . . . you shall have no other gods," an uncompromising demand uttered at the foot of the mountain.

Aaron, Moses' brother and high priest to his prophet, is often named as the embodiment of *Hod*. One wonders why. True, Exodus entrusts to Aaron the right to determine what is holy and what is commonplace and gives him exclusive authority over what is sacrificed to God on the altar in the tabernacle. It may not even be saying too much to claim that Aaron (and his descendants) controls access to the holy. From Aaron supposedly descends the line of high priests that rule the temple in Jerusalem until the Romans destroy it in 70 CE. But at the beginning, Aaron is a spectacular failure.

When Israel has arrived at Mt. Sinai and Moses has disappeared up the mountain, Israel loses its patience with Moses and Moses' God. They persuade Aaron to create for them a calf made of molten gold, and to call that calf its god. Here in the desert, when it is unclear whether Israel will trust in the one whose undying Perseverance has gotten them through the divided sea, Israel fails. Aaron fails along with them. Aaron shows no reluctance to comply with the people's demands. If anything, he guides them, engineers and oversees the project. One might argue that Aaron was just following the course of expediency, trying to keep a grumpy people happy, a babysitter mollifying a child throwing a temper tantrum. But Exodus seems to think that Aaron is more than just a coerced caregiver. Throughout the rest of the narrative, the idol is known as "the one that Aaron made."

Here is a wonder: Majesty is not pure demand, but the twinned revelation of a God who refuses to compromise on obedience and a God who constantly renews the call to obey. Perhaps the measure of Majesty is mercy—not weak, spineless, anything-goes acceptance, but forgiveness that tolerates no failure, even as it demands that we go back and try again. The narrator of Exodus never lets Aaron forget his lapse, but he also never consigns Aaron to the realms of the apostate. Aaron continues as high priest until his death, and his descendants follow him. God, it seems, refuses to let Aaron go.

. . .

Christian theology—especially the Reformed tradition—insists on what it calls the "sovereignty" of God. God alone is Lord, Reformed preachers have thundered, and God's grandeur is written into the warp and weft of creation. They have heard the echo of their preachments in the thunderstorms that rake the mountains, the crashing of waves against rocky New England shorelines, the vast tingling silences of the desert made holy by the passing of *deus absconditus*. The sovereign God brooks no opposition, permits no deviation, resists all description, answers to no name. To speak of the sovereignty of God is to stand in awe before a God who does not need us but chooses to claim us.

Not far from Abiquiu, New Mexico, is a limestone arroyo made famous by the artist Georgia O'Keefe in the late 1920s. O'Keefe called it Plaza Blanca, "the white place," for the white rock columns and cliffs that stand out in stark relief against the crystal cerulean New Mexico sky. It is an uncompromising place, a place of sharp edges and abrupt transitions. At the mouth of the arroyo is an enormous formation I call the "Dancing Sisters" because it evokes for me the memory of a group of women in traditional Mexican dresses dancing in a circle. The trail winds past the Sisters up into the arroyo through increasingly narrow passages until it reaches a dead end, hemmed in by sheer white walls over 60 feet high. Along the way, on the right is the "Cathedral," a series of hoodoos all roughly the same height that evoke the vision of a French Gothic sanctuary.

None of the spectacular rock formations that populate this canyon are the result of human manipulation. This is a place that does not need you.

The limestone formations of Plaza Blanca are sculpted by the hand of God, if one may use that metaphor, using wind and water and time itself as hammer and chisel, mute testimony to divine power and the Perseverance of Desire. Plaza Blanca is silent, eerie, and dry, baking in the New Mexico summer sun. Walk the trail up the arroyo from the Sisters to the final point where the trail narrows to nothing and disappears into the rock. Experience there an alien world, that tolerates without welcoming you, that sings songs in a language you do not understand and makes no effort to translate. This is the abode of the divine, whose Presence is always just disappearing around the next bend in the path, trailing the aroma of Majesty wafting over the canyon rim in the superheated air. This is the realm of a God whose angels are rattlesnakes, whose word is silence, and whose sovereignty pours from the clouds and cascades down the rockface in raging torrents that sweep through the arroyo without warning or mercy. If you see clouds gathering, and even if you don't, do not overstay your welcome.

At the same time, this is a place of immense, other-worldly beauty that summons you back again and again to stand in its presence and be transfigured. It refuses to release you, this sovereign Beauty, not because Beauty needs you, but because you need Beauty. It bids you return and receive again from its alien splendor even as it threatens to snuff out the very life that thrives on that splendor. The gift and the threat are not separate; they are part and parcel of the same experience.

Belden Lane says of Israel's experience in the wild desert: "Standing nakedly before the divine resplendence, they discover the indifference of God to be yet another form of God's insistent love."[2] What Israel learned in the wilderness is what any pilgrim through hostile landscapes comes to understand: that life is not wrung by force from the grasp of God but received as a gift from the open hand of the God. What Israel also learned in the wilderness is that the gift of life God gives is rarely the gift desired, but always the gift needed.

"I am the Lord your God . . . " says *Netsaḥ*, the nameless, formless essence of *'Ein Sof* expressed in shape and name. " . . . [W]ho brought you up from the land of Egypt, out of the house of slavery . . . ," declares *Netsaḥ*, God insisting that no oppression can tear those whom God delivers from the grip of that deliverance. This is the beginning of the first commandment: a promise of divine Perseverance, of *Netsaḥ*.

"You shall have no other gods before me," says *Hod*, the glory of *'Ein Sof* expressed in demand for obedience, for loyalty. "You shall have no other gods," says *Hod*, God melting all the shining idols created by the distracted delivered in the caustic heat of divine glory. This is how the first commandment ends, with the uncompromising divine demand, with *Hod*.

2. Lane, *Solace*, p.56.

Perseverance at the divided sea leads through holy deserts to the foot of the mountain of Majesty. But the Majesty at the mountain is not the end of the journey; it is the beginning. The Majesty of the mountain dispatches those who receive it down from its slopes, through other divided seas and across other holy deserts. The way is hard. The God of the Mountain is not an easy god to follow. Those who follow the way will face dangers and encounter threats too deadly to survive without the persevering deliverance of God. But they survive, because God refuses to let go.

Netsaḥ and *Hod* are one.

Cloud and Fire and Glory

In the narrative of Exodus, the people gather at the foot of Mt. Sinai in expectation of meeting at last the Cloud and Fire who divided the waters and drove them into the desert, who provided water from rocks and manna from dew, but who has remained resolutely out of reach. Hardly have they pitched their tents before the spectacle begins. "On the morning of the third day, there was thunder and lightning, as well as a thick cloud on the mountain, and a blast of a trumpet so loud that all the people who were in the camp trembled" (Ex 19:16). The mountain itself was "wrapped in smoke, because the Lord had descended on it in fire; the smoke went up like the smoke of a kiln, while the whole mountain shook violently."

And the divine-human concourse is no less stunning: "As the blast of the trumpet grew louder and louder, Moses would speak and God would answer him in thunder" (Ex 19:19).

...

There is geologic evidence to suggest that Sinai has volcanic origins. The mountain top has what vulcanologists call a ring dike, a large generally circular rock structure usually formed by the collapse of a magma chamber deep below the surface which causes the ground above it to subside, leaving behind a large cauldron-shaped space at the mountain's top—hence the name, "caldera." The subsidence of the dike is almost always the result of an eruption, in which massive clouds of ash are blasted high into the atmosphere and rain down miles from the mountain. Lava flows from the rupture down volcanic flanks in rivers of fire. The caldera collapse is often followed by steam venting from within the mountain, as though some great, ancient locomotive were releasing its brakes at the end of its journey. Rocks on and around Mt. Sinai show evidence of having originated at widely varying depths within the earth's crust, suggesting they may have been belched up in an eruption from deep within the earth.

Was the mountain erupting as Israel gathered at its foot? Perhaps, but in truth the eruption was likely less physical than metaphysical. Perhaps what happens at Sinai is the breaking forth of something held deep in the vaults of time, something inscribed not merely in the stone-cut tablets Moses brings down the mountain slope but expressed in the warp and weft of creation. Perhaps what was erupting was not magma from the bowels of the earth but Desire from the heart of God.

...

Deep within the mystical structures of the *sefirot*, *'Ein Sof* expresses itself as Desire, the will to create, to relate, to call into being the other. Desire begins the process of creation, from the primordial emptiness of *tzimtzum* to the fullness of all that is. Before *bereshith*, before there is a beginning, *'Ein Sof* issues forth a single ray of Light, a Fire, a white heat from deep within the essence of *'Ein Sof*. The Fire is the essence of *'Ein Sof*, the substance of Desire. The Fire that is Light that is *Keter* (Desire) rises like magma from the hidden chambers of *Ḥokmah* (Wisdom), *Binah* (Understanding), and *Da'at* (Knowledge); it flows like lava from the vents of *Hesed* (Love) and *Gevurah/Din* (Judgment) and erupts in *Tif'eret* (Beauty), hurled up like blazing rocks from the innermost being of God. It subsides through the insistence of *Netsaḥ* (Perseverance) and the resistance of *Hod* (Majesty) to form the caldera of *Yesod* (Foundation). Upon the foundation of *Yesod* God builds the world. *Yesod* gathers the Fire of *'Ein Sof*, connects the energies of God with the reality of the world. Upon *Yesod* rest the deep principles that define the structure of creation, rocks from the basement of time.

In the Tree of Life, in addition to the connection between the left and right "sides" of the *sefirot*, there is also a direct line that runs from *Keter* through *Da'at* to *Tif'eret* until it reaches *Yesod*. It is true of the *sefirot* that the Desire of God is expressed in the Foundation of the world. Perhaps this is why *Yesod*, a masculine noun in Hebrew, is most often characterized by the male sexual organ: because in a way mystically symbolized by human procreation, the procreation of creation begins in the Desire of the Creator.

Below *Yesod* is *Malkhuth*, or in many versions of the Tree, *Shekinah*. *Malkhuth* means "kingdom," the land dependent on and resultant from the faithful labors of the King. *Shekinah* is a Hebrew word that does not appear in the Hebrew Scriptures but rather in the Talmud, and it means "Presence." *Shekinah* is how the glory of God appears to the world, to us. *Shekinah* is the sense that there is more to be experienced, known, and inquired about God than the totality of the data our senses can provide. *Shekinah* is the mystery of God, lingering just beyond the edges of human perception, unknowable and unknown. *Shekinah* and *Malkhuth* are feminine nouns in Hebrew, giving rise to their characterization as the female organs, especially the womb. If *Yesod* is the organ of divine progeniture, *Shekinah* is the womb from which creation is born. If *Yesod* is the King who begets his children, *Malkhuth* is the realm wherein the King's children dwell. Neither can serve its function, can be itself, without the other. Without *Yesod*, Desire never reaches expression. Without *Shekinah*, Desire never culminates in creation.

. . .

"And the glory of the Lord settled on Mt. Sinai, and the cloud covered it for six days . . . the appearance of the glory was like a devouring fire . . . " (Ex. 24:16-17).

The mountain is erupting with the glory of the Lord. From deep within, deep below, deep beyond the definitions of time or space, Desire is erupting, impregnating reality with creation. Knowledge is taking shape in the Law. Beauty is rising from its rest in the heart of the divine and preparing to be known in the world. It is *Yesod,* the Foundation of all that is, the heart of the world that burns with the Fire of God.

Encircling the mountain is the Cloud. It is the Cloud that summoned Israel through the divided sea. It is the Cloud that has marked out a path through the holy deserts. It throws itself around the shoulders of the mountain like a shawl whose tassels flow down the rifts and clefts of the mountainside and dissolve on the desert floor. It is *Shekinah,* the glory of the Lord, settling onto the shoulders of Sinai, as though it were a royal robe draped about the shoulders of the King.

And the Cloud is Fire. The Fire that illumined the sea floor in the dark night of escape. The Fire that stood guard over the tents of the desert wanderers while they slept in their exhaustion. The Fire that lit the way from shore to foot of mountain. It is *Shekinah,* the glory of the Lord, an unquenchable flame that burns away all impurities and leaves behind only that which is true.

. . .

In a tiny Galilean town, a woman has a vision. "Greetings, favored one," says a figure who is not quite God but much more than she. "The Lord is with you." Mary is even now bearing a child, and the stories say the child is the essence of the Desire of God. "The Holy Spirit will come upon you, and the power of the Most High will overshadow you; therefore the child to be born will be holy; he will be called the Son of God" (Luke 1:35). The Holy takes on shape and substance in Mary's womb. But do not think that Mary's only value is as a vessel of the holy. Mary is more than a walking womb, a ready urn for containing Desire. She is co-creator of the creation, the one through whom glory becomes visible. In Christian story, perhaps the Holy Spirit is *Yesod,* the Foundation of the world, the truth on which creation rests. If so, then Mary is *Shekinah,* the bearer of glory. She is the hope of the world. From her will erupt a new creation.

...

Moses, the narrator of Exodus tells us, comes down from the mountain a changed man for his encounter with God. Whatever invisible changes of heart or mind he may have experienced, one change is visible to all: "the skin of his face shone because he had been talking with God" (Ex. 34:30). Imagination suggests that no one stands long in the presence of the divine Fire without bursting into flame and being set alight.

THE CORD

Joshua 2:1–21

Everything depends upon the cord.

. . .

The story of Israel's entry into and settlement of Canaan begins at Jericho. As the story goes, Joshua, Moses' lieutenant and successor, sends two men into Jericho as a reconnaissance party, to spy on the city's defenses behind its legendary impregnable walls. Their first stop upon gaining entry is the house of Rahab, whom the English translations call a "prostitute" (*'ishah zonah*). It isn't long before news of their arrival is coursing through town, leading to a visit to Rahab by soldiers from Jericho's ruler. Rahab, however, has come to believe that Israelite conquest of Jericho is inevitable, and wanting the be on the right side of history she hides the spies under piles of flax on her roof. When the soldiers have gone, she lowers the spies over the city wall by rope and bids them hide for three days before returning to Joshua. Before they go, she extracts from them the promise that she and her family will be spared in the carnage following Jericho's fall. She and the spies agree that the sign that her house is to remain unmolested in the fight is the rope—"this crimson cord"—by which she has conveyed the spies themselves to safety. The spies urge upon her the importance of the act: in the fog of war, those in the wrong places die. If she forgets the cord, they forget their promise. Her deliverance depends upon the crimson cord tied in her window.

. . .

Other cords, other promises.

Long before Rahab and her spies, Judah—son of Jacob and eventual eponym for a nation—visits the tent of a woman he takes to be a prostitute (again, *zonah*, Gen 38:15). He does not recognize her, but she is his daughter-in-law Tamar, widow of his deceased eldest son Er. Upon Er's death, Judah gave to her his second son, Onan, whose legal responsibility was to take Tamar as his wife and have children with her, a way of preserving the lineage of his brother. Onan, however, resists, and practices the oldest form of birth control. Onan's resistance angers God, who slays the rebellious Onan. Judah has a third son, Shelah, but Judah fears that Shelah will meet a similar fate—perhaps Tamar is a sort of "black widow?"—and so denies Tamar her chance at children and sends her back to her father's house, damaged goods returned to seller in the harsh economy of ancient marriage. Years later, after the death of his own wife, Judah feels the ancient stirrings and decides to visit the tent of someone who ostensibly knows what to do with them. In exchange, the woman demands a price: a new kid, the offspring of one of his herd. But Judah is traveling light; he has no livestock with him. The best he can do is to give her a pledge, betokened by his staff, and his cord. And so does Tamar become pregnant with the children of her father-in-law.

Children, because in the grand plot of divine irony, Tamar is pregnant with male twins, infant replacements of Judah's lost sons, second chances at a future. When the pregnancy is revealed, Tamar identifies the father with the staff and cord given to her at the time of her conception. It is a moment of incredible risk to Tamar. If Judah denies the staff and cord, denies his paternity, Tamar is branded for life and cast out from the polite society of the righteous. If he accepts the children, Judah seems a lecherous old fool. But casting aside fears of embarrassment, Judah acknowledges that the children are his own and that, far from being immoral and sexually irresponsible, Tamar is more righteous than he. She has held to the law of lineage, even as he tried to abrogate it.

But the tale is not fully told. At last comes the moment for Tamar to deliver. As the story goes, the twins struggle within the womb for the right of primogeniture. One manages to reach a hand out from the womb, and the midwife marks him as firstborn by tying around his wrist a bit of crimson thread. Imagination wonders if it is the very cord that had been proof of his parentage. His brother pulls him back and emerges first—a "breach" says the midwife, and the source of his name, Perez—but the cord on his brother's wrist illumines the truth. The second to emerge is the first to be born, by the light of the cord around his wrist. His name is Zerah, "brightness."

...

Somewhere early in the 1900s, and perhaps earlier, a practice emerged within Jewish mystical folklore. The believer who felt imperiled by evil forces tied a crimson or scarlet thread around the left wrist, carefully knotted with seven knots. The crimson cord was thought to protect its wearer from the "evil eye." Like many such superstitions, the meaning has been hollowed out of the shell of its practice as it has moved out into wider social and cultural contexts; nowadays celebrities who dabble in mystical and occult practices are often seen wearing them as a fashion accessory. Not unlike, one suspects, the use of the cross as ornamental jewelry.

...

Other cords, other deliverances.

In the early days of the Christian church, Saul—who is better known by his Latin name, Paul—is a noted persecutor of Christians. On his way from Jerusalem to Damascus, as the story goes, he is overcome by an intense light and has a vision of Jesus. The vision leaves Saul temporarily blind and changes his attitude about the nascent faith of the followers of Jesus. Brought by his traveling companions to Damascus, Saul is taken in by Ananias, a member of the Damascene Christian community. Saul—now Paul—becomes Ananias's student, learning the faith from him. His reputation as a preacher and teacher begins to grow, attracting attention not only from Christian admirers but also from those who resist his teaching or do not trust his conversion. A plot to kill him seems to have hatched but been discovered, and Paul escapes, lowered from a window in the Damascus city walls in a basket suspended by a rope. Given his importance as evangelist, theologian, and author of a large portion of the Christian New Testament, it seems no exaggeration to say that the future of one of the world's great religions depends on that rope.

...

Other cords, other symbols.

The book of Ecclesiastes, famous for its hard-nosed realism about the human prospect and yet also its curiously understated confidence in the enduring goodness of God, ends with a poem about death (Ecc 12:1–8).

"Remember your creator in the days of your youth," the poet adjures the reader, "before the days of trouble come. . .."

For millenia, interpreters of the poem have associated its imagery with various parts of the human body as they fail in advancing age. The "guards of the house" that "tremble" are supposedly the rib cage; the "strong men" who are "bent" are the legs. "[T]he women who grind cease working" seems an image of aged teeth, and "those who look through the windows see dimly" seems to describe fading sight. The "almond tree" with its white blossoms evokes white hair atop elderly heads, and the "grasshopper" that "drags itself along" seems to suggest sexual dysfunction and loss of desire. Metaphor tumbles upon metaphor as the poem proceeds, each pointing to another sign of creeping decrepitude, inching ever closer to oblivion, when ". . . all must go to their eternal home, and the mourners will go about in the streets . . . ."

At the last, says the Teacher, "the silver cord is snapped, and the golden bowl is broken, and the pitcher is broken at the fountain, and the wheel is broken at the cistern, and the dust returns to the earth as it was, and the breath returns to God who gave it." Traditionally, these last images have been understood as figures for death. One stands out: "the silver cord is snapped." Imagination suggests the metaphor of a silver cord that connects the living with life itself, so that when it is "snapped" the connection is severed, and death is the result.

. . .

Christian hymnody, and especially English hymnody, celebrates the unity of believers in Christ. The hymn "In Christ There Is No East or West" includes this stanza:

> In Christ shall true hearts everywhere
> their high communion find;
> his service is the golden cord
> close binding humankind.

. . .

Other cords, other connections.

Gershom Scholem, in his *Major Trends in Jewish Mysticism*, writes of Isaac Luria's belief that hope for the restoration of creation to the creative intent of *'Ein Sof* rested principally on the prayers of the faithful. Luria, Scholem argues, saw prayer as the means by which the soul might end its long imprisonment in flesh in the realm of evil and brokenness, and find hope for liberation and reunion with its Creator.

> The individual's prayers, as well as those of the community, but particularly the latter, are under certain conditions the vehicle of the soul's mystical ascent to God. The words of prayer, more particularly the traditional liturgical prayer with its fixed text, *become a silken cord with the aid of which the mystical intention of the mind gropes its dangerous way through the darkness towards God*" (p. 276, emphasis added).[1]

. . .

The cord is more than a rope hung from a window to let down a load. It is the cord that permits the past to escape into the future. It is more than a plea for safety; it is a promise of inclusion. It is more than a means of entrapment; it is a guarantee of rightful place. It is more than a means of descent; it is an ascent to God. It is more than a token of exchange; it is sign of belonging. It is more than a form of bondage; it is the bond of unity. It is more than a cry for help. It is the currency of hope.

Everything depends upon the cord.

---

1. Gershom Scholem, *Major Trends in Jewish Mysticism*. New York: Schocken Books, 1945, 1995, p. 276.

Shevirah—The Shattering

There is a crisis within the Infinite, a crisis that spills over into the whole creation. The crisis is the brokenness of things.

Isaac Luria grounded his mythic vision of creation in the absolute perfection of the unity of *'Ein Sof*. From that perfect unity, there ought to have come a creation that was also perfect. But it wasn't perfect; it was in fact deeply broken. Luria thus confronted the same dilemma that every theologian faces: how to explain the origins of evil, suffering, and brokenness. Luria did not have the option—as indeed no serious theologian from among the Western traditions has ever had—of blaming evil and suffering on some demiurge, an alternate deity in competition with the Infinite, a devil to accuse for perfection's demise. Such a proposal would constitute polytheism and fly in the face of Israel's core commitment: "Hear, O Israel, the Lord your God, the Lord is One" (Deut 6:4). There "is" "only" the Infinite. Rather, he must explain the origins of evil from within the reality of the Infinite.

Luria's response was to return to the notion of the *sefirot*, the ten emanations of the Infinite. He began with the Light that falls from the Infinite in the immediate aftermath of *tzimtzum*. He imagined that the Light enters the emptiness created by *tzimtzum* and immediately begins to move in various geometric patterns: whorls and circles and angles and lines in stunning, limitless variety. Imagine a grand, infinite fireworks display, with lights fizzing and whirling, shooting and curling, exploding and illumining the eternal darkness with colors and shapes. Gradually, these varying patterns of the Light gather to form the *sefirot*, each one different because of the different peculiar movements of the Light in the emptiness. One by one, the *sefirot* take on spiritual form and substance and position themselves in relation to each other, forming the Tree of Life.

In the earliest moments, Luria imagined, the Light coalesces into "vessels"—the Hebrew term is *kelim*—whose purpose is to receive the Light. Once formed, each vessel begins to fill with the pure Light of the Infinite, as water fills a bowl held under a stream. Imagination suggests a sort of cosmic water sculpture, the divine light first forming and then filling each vessel, and then overflowing and spilling down to form and fill the next and the next.

But here is where the crisis occurs. The vessels of the lower seven *sefirot*, as they fill with Light, become unstable. They crack, then split, and finally shatter. The shards of the broken *sefirot* fall from their place. Some of the Light, now fragmented and shattered, returns to the Infinite, while other shards of the Light fall to a lower realm and are trapped there. Luria calls this cataclysm *shevirat-hakelim*, the shattering of the vessels, or simply *shevirah*, shattering. He regards this as the central crisis in the life of the Infinite.

Think of this for a moment. The Infinite wills the emanations through the overflow of Desire, and yet the structure of those emanations fails. What does it mean that the Infinite sets out to bring something into being, and fails in the attempt? What does it mean that God fails?

And how? How can the Infinite fail? If there exists nothing that resists the Infinite, then how does the Infinite's Desire *not* come perfectly into being? And if there is something that resists the Desire of the Infinite, where does it come from?

...

In the myths of human origin, especially in Genesis 2 and 3, God creates a world that perfectly reflects divine intent. A garden paradise illumined by sun and moon, watered by rivers that flow from its center, populated by the creatures of God's imagination, crowned by the man and the woman. These latter are limited by only one restriction: they must not eat of the tree of the knowledge of good and evil. Everything is in its place, and all is good. Relational perfection reigns: the man and the woman are naked, before God and each other, and are not ashamed.

Enter the serpent, "more crafty" than any other creature sprung from God's Desire. The serpent is not, mind you, more evil or more sinful. It is craftier—as though it has a set of skills the equal of which is possessed by none other of the creatures of the garden. Craftiness is the serpent being the serpent, as God created it. The serpent, like every other creature in the garden, is the expression of the creative Desire of God. The serpent is good because God imagined it into being. And being nothing other than the creature of God's imagination, the serpent poses the question that lies at the heart of every decision to obey: "Are you sure?"

It's hard to know which came first: our fear of snakes or our sense that they are inherently evil. But nothing in the narrative suggests that the serpent is evil; only that it is willing to ask the question no one else is bold enough to ask. It is as though the serpent is the part of God willing to suggest that decisions to obey might best be preceded by a bit of critical thinking.

. . .

Among the *sefirot*, those on the "left" side of the Tree—*Binah, Gevurah/Din,* and *Hod*— contribute structure, judgment, and resistance to the flow of Desire, even as insight and love and persistence from the Tree's "right" side press it forward. It is as though, in the very essence of the Infinite, there is a series of little dams to impede the flow of Desire, each challenging Desire as it flows toward creation, each asking in its own way, are you sure?

Luria saw these elements of resistance and judgment as both necessary and problematic. In the largest sense, Luria knew, these structuring elements were essential to bring creation into being. But inherent within the resistance they offer to Desire is the potential for disobedience of the divine command, an unwillingness to go with Desire's creative flow. Luria could not escape the idea that deep within the being of the Infinite is located that which might become rebellion against the Infinite—evil.

That is what the *tzimtzum* is for, either he or his disciples reasoned: to purge the Infinite of those negative, resistant, potentially evil elements of the essence of the Infinite that might one day rebel against the Infinite. Pour them out into vessels wherein they might be contained, away from the purity of divine Desire. Quarantine them until they have lost their power to hurt or destroy.

When the *tzimtzum* occurred, said Luria, the emptiness created was not truly empty. Imagine a glass full of water, he suggested. When the water is emptied out, some residue of water remains inside the glass, clinging to the sides. *Reshimu*, "remnant" or "residue," he called it. The *reshimu* is the negative energy within the being of the Infinite. It is the Infinite; it is not some other, alien, opposed deity. But it is the Infinite seeking to challenge, resist, and undo itself. When the Light is poured into the emptiness and begins to form the vessels of the *sefirot*, some of that residue is mixed with the Light, more in the lower *sefirot* than in the higher, and thus they are weaker, less able to contain the power of the Light. They shatter, and the Light is fractured, some ascending to the Infinite, and some remaining in the dark realms of brokenness below.

Again, such insights arise from this image! The origin of the brokenness of the world is *in the Infinite*. The failure of Infinite's creation can be traced to the failure of its Creator. In creating, the Infinite imbues creation with imperfections that come from within the Infinite. Good and evil, so starkly different in our conceptions of the divine, are one in the Infinite.

In the shattering of the *sefirot*, God is shattered, broken, scattered amid the fragments of the world.

. . .

We know what it is to live in the dark realms of brokenness, with only flashes of Light dimly reflected. We know what it is to live in the realms of shadow, where truths are half-glimpsed, and fear governs the world we see when we close our eyes. We know what it is to live with seething hatred, love ingrown upon itself, turned sick and self-centered. We know what it is to construct systems intended to make justice, only to have them perpetuate injury and wrong. We know what it is to die, even as we live. "Wretched man that I am," once cried Paul, "who will rescue me from this body of death?" (Rom 7:24).

The Hebrew prophets lived with an abiding sense of the disappointment of God with human lives and creation God intended for better:

> For the vineyard of the Lord of hosts is the house of Israel,
> > and the people of Judah are his pleasant planting;
> he expected justice, but saw bloodshed,
> > righteousness, but heard a cry! (Isa 5:7)

Justice and bloodshed, righteousness and an outcry. Sometimes the two are deceptively similar: "justice" in Hebrew is *mishpat*, while "bloodshed" is *mishpaḥ*; "righteousness" is *tzedakah*, while "cry" is *tzeʿaqah*. Say them aloud and listen to the assonance between them. Sometimes the distance from good to evil is not so very far at all.

The inclination is to read Isaiah's words as a condemnation of human injustice and inhumanity, and indeed, so it is. But is there more? If God's creation is broken, is God broken, too? The Light that falls into creation is the Light of the Infinite, born of Desire and expressing itself in the emanations of the *sefirot*. If the Light that falls from Desire into the darkness has failed in its effort to create its intended perfection and now is trapped amid the fragments of its disaster, is God also trapped, imprisoned in the darkness and brokenness, unable to be God? Is the crisis of *shevirah* not merely that the world becomes a shattered world, but that God becomes a shattered God?

The Shining Darkness

After the Shattering comes the darkness.

According to Luria, once the lower *sefirot* have shattered, the shards fall into a realm of deep darkness, a place where Light and the hope it gives are foreign, unknown. Luria refers to the shards of the *sefirot* as *kelippot*—"husks" or "shells"—a name to convey, it seems, their barrenness and failure. Instead of bearing their intended fruit, they are hollowed, fractured, and dry. In their broken, fallen state, they form a realm of destruction and rebelliousness, the realm into which creation is plunged and in which we continue to live. The realm is *tehiru*, "chaos," related to the term *tehom*, "the deep," in Gen 1:2 that describes the formless, orderless condition of the world before creation.

But even now, even in the wake of this crisis in the being of God, all is not lost. When the *sefirot* shatter and fall, some of the divine Light returns to God, but not all. Some of the Light that composed the *sefirot* remains with them as they fall. The Light is entrapped in the darkness, but not, it seems, destroyed by it. There remains Light, even in the deepest of darkness, and to borrow from the Gospel of John, "the darkness has not overcome it."

. . .

The paschal vigil begins in darkness. It is a darkness at the end of things, a darkness that vanquishes hope. The powers of death, wielded by a ruthless empire, have overwhelmed the Light, shattering the one whom John calls "the Light of the world."

Holy Saturday—the Day Between, after the crucifixion of Jesus but before the resurrection—tends to get short shrift in Christian imagination. There is, without doubt, a sort of emotional exhaustion that sets in after watching Jesus die that unutterably horrible death, seeing his lifeless body lowered from its post of execution and sealed in a convenient tomb. Whatever spiritual energy remains after the pathos of death is banked like embers from yesterday's fire, secure against the need to rekindle our passions when Easter morning dawns.

Holy Saturday is a sort of grand caesura in the music of the Passion, a silence amid the passage from palm to passion to pascha. And like a rest in a musical passage, it was meant to be observed no less than the notes around it. But what happens in this Great Silence?

The day is a day of darkness and dead ends. Jesus' body is sealed in the bowels of the tomb, and the spirits of those who love and follow him are no less entombed. To be in Holy Saturday is to be suspended in darkness. All that we have valued, loved, believed, trusted, and yearned for is shattered, broken. The cold remains of hope are wrapped in burial cloths, packed with spices to tamp down the stench of decay, and consigned to the earth's deepest darkness. The furious activity of the week grinds to a halt, and there is no movement, no sound, no word. No Light.

There is always a tendency to euphemize this moment, as though one could by choosing milder terminology soften the blow of death. But there is no softening of it. The body is not "laid to rest," as though it has dozed for a while to awaken refreshed; it is entombed, consigned to the end of the end of the end. There is no back door to the tomb, no escape hatch, no secret panel that slides aside revealing an underground passage back to life.

Holy Saturday demands to be taken seriously for what it is. It is the end. End of the story, end of the line, end of the possibility that tomorrow will be better than today. That's the thing about death: beyond it lies no tomorrow.

What does it mean to reach the end? What is it like to arrive at the place from which there is no going forward and no turning back? What does it mean to dwell in this day of darkness without the expectation of light? At least part of what it means to dwell in death is to surrender the expectation that, if we just hold on and keep our chins up, if we just click the heels of the ruby slippers and say the magic words, we will be whisked away back to the world of the-way-it-was-before. But in the tomb, there are no magic words. There are no words at all.

But if there are no words, there is the Possible. It is not a possibility we shape with our words, or even create out of the resources of our imaginations. It is a Possible discontinuous with any we can speak of, think of, imagine. And precisely because it is not a possibility of our own creation, it is the infinite Possible, unbound by the encumbrance of human events and the burden of human limitation. It is the unexpectable Possible. In perhaps the deepest irony Christian faith has to offer, Holy Saturday is the last pregnant day of Possible. Good Friday's hopes and fears are dead. Easter Sunday's joys and resolutions are unimaginable. In the darkness and silence and eternality of the tomb on Holy Saturday, everything is Possible, including nothing at all.

The Second Day

Do not yet roll the stone away
nor hurry toward tomorrow's dawn;
let us dwell in death today.

Other voices have their say
outside this sabbatic tomb.
Do not yet roll the stone away

nor come to gloat, embalm, or pray,
lament, or raise the victor's song—
let us dwell in death today.

Build no castles made of clay,
draw up no plans for sacred rooms.
Do not yet roll the stone away

and prematurely birth the day
when knowledge preens and error looms.
Let us dwell in death today:

the Possible in its unknown way
will use the dark to make us strong.
Do not yet roll the stone away,
but let us dwell in death today.[1]

Holy Saturday is holy mystery. It is the end of all limited possibilities and the beginning of the truly limitless Possible. Until Easter dawns and the resurrection illumines our sight and the unexpected becomes the real—until that moment the darkness of the tomb retains the full panoply of the

---

1. Paul K Hooker, *Days and Times: Poems from the Liturgy of Living*. Eugene, OR: Resource Publications, 2018.

Possible. This is the new Sabbath, the rest at the end of creation before the new creation begins.

The psalmist, contemplating the meaning of his own death (" . . . if I make my bed in Sheol . . . ") affirms,

> If I say, "Surely the darkness will cover me
> > and the light around me become night,"
> even the darkness is not dark to you;
> > the night is as bright as the day
> > for darkness is as light to you. (Psalm 139:11–12).

The anonymous, late 5th–early 6th c. Christian theologian known to moderns as Pseudo-Dionysius the Areopagite (or, more simply, Denys) begins his *Mystical Theology* with a poem, a paean of praise to God:

> Trinity!! Higher than any being,
> > any divinity, any goodness,
> > > Guide of Christians
> > > > in the wisdom of heaven!
> Lead us up beyond knowing and light,
> > up to the farthest, highest peak
> > > of mystic scripture,
> > where the mysteries of God's word
> > > lie simple, absolute and unchangeable
> > > in the brilliant darkness of a hidden silence.
> > Amid the deepest shadow
> > > they pour overwhelming light
> > > on what is most manifest.
> > Amid the wholly unsensed and unseen
> > > they completely fill our sightless minds
> > > with treasures beyond all beauty.[2]

Denys takes as his theological project an effort to get behind and beneath and beyond all the affirmations of faith that populate religious conversation, until he reaches a place where words and the notions they symbolize all fall away. The way to God, he believes, must eventually arrive in darkness, in a place where eyes cannot pretend they see nor minds pretend they comprehend. Denys understood that God is beyond knowing, beyond the sort of

---

2. ———, The Mystical Theology, in *Pseudo-Dionysius: The Complete Works*, trans. Colm Luibheid. Manhattan: Paulist, 1978,

certainties we rely on to compose what we think of as Truth. True certainties—the "simple, absolute and unchangeable" mysteries—are not available for inspection by the light of human reason but clothed in the cloud and darkness that forever shrouds the being of God. But, like Luria's *tehiru*, and perhaps like the inner sanctum of the Tomb, it is no hopeless darkness, but "a brilliant darkness." It is a darkness in which the soul's vision fails, but where shine, even if invisible to us, "treasures beyond all beauty."

A brilliant darkness. A darkness full of inconceivable Beauty. A death that ends every possibility and a Possible that lives after everything ends. A dark Light that enlightens darkness. A shining darkness, wherein dwells the God of the Possible.

The Light yet shines in the darkness. The darkness has not overcome it.

Atonement—The Hole in the Heart of God

Mark 15:34

In the Gospel of Mark, it is said, all roads lead to the Cross.

Mark (and Matthew who depends on Mark's narrative) places on the lips of the dying Jesus the first verse of Psalm 22, rendered in Aramaic: *'Eloi, 'Eloi, lema' sabacthani*—My God, my God, why have you abandoned me?" On the cross, the dying Jesus experiences the withdrawal of God, the "Father" with whom he has felt union and oneness throughout the arc of the gospel narrative. Jesus experiences God's abandonment in the moment he needed God's presence most of all.

For Christians, the moment of the death of Jesus is the crucial moment, the climax of the gospel story—indeed, the climactic moment of the story of God's engagement with creation. This is the moment when the work of Jesus is fulfilled, when he renders up his life in the service of the ultimate act of God's love for the world. But in this moment, we are shown not a God who overpowers evil with a show of divine strength, but one who succumbs to evil in a show of divine weakness. This is God, sacrificing God's self for the world God cares so much for. If, as Christian theology holds, Jesus is fully God even as he is also fully human, then this moment is quite literally God rending open the very fabric of the divine being, God tearing God's self apart for the sake of the world.

The hole in the heart of God.

. . .

At the beginning of the beginning of the beginning, Jewish mysticism imagines, the Infinite makes a space within the Infinite into which might come into being all that was not infinite. The *tzimtzum* is the Infinite tearing itself open, withdrawing within and from itself, pulling itself back into itself. It is the Infinite abandoning Infinity and becoming finite, abandoning limitlessness and becoming limited. At the beginning of the beginning of the beginning, the Infinite begins a process of *becoming*, of ceasing to be the Infinite and becoming God the Creator. And as God becomes God, so also does all that is not God become all that it is. The whole of creation comes into being within the emptiness created by *tzimtzum*, all darkness and light, all sea and dry land, all plants and animals and humans *in imago Dei*. The empty space is infinitesimally small and incomprehensibly large; it contains nothing at all and all there is.

Imagine that *tzimtzum* is not a once-for-all-time event in the dark mists before time, but an ongoing, eternal, and always-in-every-time reality in the mythic realm of imagination. Imagine that the Infinite is always infinite, and yet always becoming God. Imagine that the empty space created in *tzimtzum* is always and eternally being created, and that a new reality is always and eternally coming into being. Imagine that the existence of everything depends upon the eternal coming-into-being that can only happen in the timeless emptiness of *tzimtzum*. In every moment, and beyond and outside all moments, God is eternally making a hole in the heart of God.

. . .

Two millennia before Isaac Luria posited *tzimtzum*, Plato was thinking about emptiness. In *Timaeus*, that fabulous and fantastical dialogue about the creation of the world, Plato muses about the elements of creation. First are the eternal Forms, those perfect ideals of all that is, the ultimate and true reality, the union with which is the quest of all human knowledge. Second are the impermanent, ever-changing things available to be seen and touched and smelled, the imperfect copies of the eternal forms, shadows of the true reality, the perception of which is a matter of what Plato called "opinion" and "sense." These elements are related, as Plato understood them. As a crass example of that relationship, imagine a parlor in a house in which there are several objects upon which it is customary for people to sit. One is a large, vinyl-covered bag filled with dried beans; another a wood-framed structure with a wicker seat; and still a third is a large, thickly cushioned and upholstered object with plush arms and a high back. Although dramatically different in size, construction, color, and shape, they are all nonetheless recognizable to our senses as "chairs," even if we might differ in our opinion of how successfully they work as such. But what allows us to so recognize them? Plato suggests it is the existence of the eternal form of "chair" in whose reality all the imperfect, differing, and varyingly successful physical "copies" of chairs participate.

But how, Plato seems to wonder, does the eternal ideal Form become the impermanent sensate copy? How do sensate copies participate in the eternal ideals? Plato has no answer, at least not one that satisfies his own rigorous logic. Instead, he depends on mysticism. The transition takes place, he argues, in a third element: a space that provides a place wherein all that is comes into being. The space—Plato's word is *chora,* which elsewhere in Greek can mean anything from "mother" to "nurse" to "receptacle"—is not a "place" so much as the absence of place, not "being" so much as the precondition for becoming. Plato's description of the element of space is fascinating:

> Space exists always and cannot be destroyed. It provides a location for all things that come to be. It is itself apprehended by a kind of bastard reasoning that does not involve sense perception, and it is hardly even an object of conviction. We look at it as in a dream when we say that everything must of necessity be somewhere, and that that which is neither on earth nor anywhere in heaven is nothing.[1]

Forms, which are eternal ideals, take on corporeality—imperfect and transitory—in the "space" which is neither form nor corpus. The space is neither in "heaven"—the realm of the Forms—nor on earth—the realm of corporeality. It is thus "nothing." It defies logic and description, resists categorization, and is thus "apprehended by a kind of bastard reasoning" that is neither logic nor sensibility but more like a dream, something fleeting and just out of reach. And yet this unreachable, unknowable, indefinable third element is the essential intermediary by which intangible Form is made over into tangibility. It is, imagination suggests, very much like the emptiness of *tzimtzum*. An emptiness in the heart of God which is not-God and within which all that is comes to be and without which nothing that is could come to be. *Chora*—the space—holds the whole world.

Plato's noun *chora* — "space"—has a verb form: *chorein,* "to make space for." Those who have spent time dwelling with Trinitarian theology know immediately the significance of that shift from noun to verb: *chorein* is the root form of *perichorein*, meaning to "make room for each other." Since the work of John of Damascus in the eighth century, Christians have used this

---

1. Plato, *Timaeus*, trans. Donald J. Zeyl., *Complete Works*, ed. John M. Cooper. Indianapolis: Hackett, 1997, p 1255.

verb and its nominal form *perichoresis* to describe the relationship of the three persons of the Trinity: Father, Son and Spirit—Lover, Beloved, and Love, Desirer, Desired, and Desire. The Three, it is said, are in such relationship that the presence of any one is the presence of all three. Constantly interwoven and inter-penetrating each other, they are in such essential unity that, though distinct from one another, they are inseparable from one another. Eternally and always, in every moment and beyond all moments, they are making room for one another, eternally and always inhabiting each other's space. *Perichoresis*. At the heart of this relationship is space, *chora*, the emptiness that is full of the other.

...

Nowhere is that emptiness more apparent, more poignant, than in the moment Jesus dies on the cross. In the heart of the moment is space, or what theologian William Placher once called "distance within God":

> We trust that the distance between Jesus crying out in abandonment on the cross and the one he had always before called his Father mirrors some sort of distance within God—thought we cannot imagine what terms like "distance within God" can mean. A kind of space lies within the triune God—a space potentially inclusive of the space of sinners and doubters—and yet this space is no desert but a spiritual garden of mutual love and glorification. In the incarnation, the three show that there is always within God a space large enough for the whole world, and even all its sin: The Word's distance from the one he calls Father is so great that no one falls outside it, and the Spirit fills all that space with love.[2]

Christians perhaps think of Jesus' death on the cross as a moment in history, a one-time event, and indeed, the cross is certainly an event in time and place. But is it more? Is it also a moment out-of-time, out-of-place, eternally and always occurring in the mystery of the Infinite? Imagine that the *tzimtzum* of the cross is an event in eternity, eternally and always occurring within the Infinite, bringing into being an emptiness within which is gathered all the brokenness of the world, all the shattered vessels of divine Desire, all the Light trapped in the darkness. Imagine that in the eternal emptiness there is always occurring the birth of a new creation, the

---

2. William Placher, *The Triune God: Essays in Postliberal Theology.* Louisville: Westminster John Knox, 2007, p.155.

potential for the unexpectable possibility of life. Imagine that eternally and always is occurring the coming-into-being of God, distant and divided and distinct, and yet united and inseparable.

...

According to Mark, after he cries *'Eloi, 'Eloi, lema' sabacthani* from the cross, "Jesus gave a loud cry and breathed his last." In Mark, these are the last words Jesus speaks, the last sounds he utters. With this last cry, he dies. After he dies, there is silence.

Imagination enters the Silence. The Silence is Empty. The darkness is complete. No Light falls from beyond the stars. No Word echoes in the darkness. There is no Death, for dying is done. There is no Life, for living is not yet begun. Nothing is happening here, for there are no things to act. The Silence is Empty, and the Emptiness is Silent.

And yet the Emptiness is full of Possibility. Not the extension of plans already in place in human minds or hearts, not the extrapolation of the pattern of human events. A Possibility so completely disjoined from all that has gone before as to be utterly unexpectable. A Possibility so unique as to be unknown and unknowable. A Possibility so infinitesimally small as to be unnoticeable; a Possibility so infinitely grand as to include the whole shattered, broken world.

The Possibility draws unto itself all the brokenness of the world, all the shattered fragments of the Light, the ragged visions and dented dreams, tatterdemalions of a fractured creation. The Possibility gathers in the darkness all the evil and the wrong, all the failed efforts and flawed intent, all the love soured into hatred, all the hope curdled into fear. The Possibility gathers them all, as though a bird gathering its young beneath its wings. And it waits.

The Possibility is born of Desire, the same Desire that moves within the innermost parts of the Infinite at the beginning of the beginning of the beginning. The same Desire that expresses itself as Wisdom and structures itself as Understanding. The same Desire that bursts forth as Love and disciplines itself as Judgment. The same Desire that is Beauty. The Possibility is the Beauty of the Infinite. The Beauty waits in the Silence, in the Emptiness, in the shining darkness.

Tikkun—Light, Love, Repair

The gospel stories do not permit us into the tomb on Holy Saturday, nor in the wee hours of the Day of Resurrection, before the dawn. When the tomb is sealed with the great stone at the end of the Good Friday drama, Jesus vanishes into the darkness and silence of death. We will see him no more as we have known him. The story is over.

The vigil draws our attention elsewhere, to other stories told on this night to teach us the meaning of his life and dying. From the *bereshith* of the beginning, to the shore of the divided sea, across the deserts and to the foot of the mountain, through the life of the people formed by Word and Fire, to the agony of the cross and the resignation of the tomb, the stories work their magic, make us part of their world, their life. But at last they deposit us here, outside the tomb, as though a guided tour through a cavern has come to its end and the guide has bid us farewell at the cavemouth where we began. Time to get in the car and head for home.

But like a child whose imagination has been fired by a hole in the earth older than he can imagine, who has witnessed the wonder of stalagmites and stalactites, organ-pipe rocks that resonate with deep notes rumbling in the basement of time, we are reluctant to leave. This cannot be the end. The story cannot end like this. There must be more.

...

The drama of creation, as Isaac Luria portrayed it, has three acts. First is *tzimtzum*, the self-rending of the Infinite that makes possible all things. Second is *shevirah*, the shattering that breaks creation, but also breaks God. The third is *tikkun*, the repair.

Luria understood the whole story of Israel as God's attempt to overcome the crisis of *shevirah*, to undo the damage of the catastrophic failure of the *sefirot*. It is a story of successive efforts at redemption, and the failure of each one in turn. The creation of Adam and Eve in the garden is intended to be a place of perfection and wholeness, but the man and woman choose disobedience instead. The call to Abraham is intended to be the foundation of a nation faithful to God, but Abraham's trust in the promise of that nation is irresolute and wavering. The Cloud and Fire atop the mountain should have been the dramatic moment when Israel comes to know its God through the gift of Torah, but instead the people look away in fear and make for themselves a golden calf. Joshua leads the people across the Jordan and into Canaan, but once there the people find the lusciousness of worshiping of Ba'al more attractive than the austerity of faithfulness to God. Again and again, down through history, a new creation, a new Light. Again and again, the vessels prove too weak, and a new shattering. David and the kingdom. Exile and the destruction of the Temple. Judah the Maccabee and the magical cruse of oil. Herod and Rome and the ruin of the second Temple. On and on and on. New creation, new catastrophe.

One wonders why, with such a record, God continues to try. But here we reach the profoundest irony of Jewish mysticism. God has no other choice. The crisis in the being of God that leads to *shevirah,* to the shattering, is internal to God and not self-correcting. If the brokenness of the world is to be overcome, humans are the essential agents of its overcoming. God who creates the world creates human life to repair creation.

Every act of obedience, Luria argued, every hour spent in study of Torah, every recitation of a prayer, every deed of kindness, every act of justice and mercy—of *mishpat* and *tsedaqah*—is an act of *tikkun,* of repair. Each time the faithful person acts in a way that reflects the divine Light in the world, a fragment of the Light still trapped in the darkness of *tehiru* is lifted from its entrapment and returns to the Giver of Light. Because evil thrives on the divine energy of the Light it holds in the darkness, the release of the Light weakens evil. One day—and no one knows when—the last entrapped fragment of the Light will be released, and evil will cease to be.

So much depends on us! We humans bear enormous responsibility for *tikkun,* for the repair of the world. We are co-creators of a restored creation, co-achievers of the divine intent. Every act of justice or kindness or faithfulness might be the act that frees the Light and restores the world. Every one of us, and all of us together, are presented every day in every moment with an opportunity to participate in making the world whole. We fail; God help us, we fall beneath this holy burden. But beside us are others who will share the weight, who assist us to our feet and redistribute the load. A persistent God calls us to *tikkun.* A majestic God refuses our failures and renews the opportunity again.

Jesus says to his disciples:

> I give you a new commandment, that you love one another. Just as I have loved you, you also should love one another. By this everyone will know that you are my disciples, if you have love for one another (John 13:34-35).

and later, in a prayer to the one he calls Father, he prays . . .

> . . . that they may be one, as we are one, I in them and you in me, that they may become completely one, so that the world may know that you have sent me and have loved them even as you have loved me (John 17:22b-23).

To be a disciple is to love. To be one with God, to heal some portion of the brokenness of creation, is to love. The repair of the world depends on love.

. . .

In the beginning of the beginning of the beginning, the Infinite overflows with Desire, with the Love that is the Infinite. Desire, Love, is as deep and broad and high as is the Infinite. It is all there is. As there "is" "only" the Infinite, there is only Love.

And Love is made flesh, and dwells among us. One of us.

In the Silence and the Emptiness of *tzimtzum,* Desire eternally begins anew. The energy of Desire receives the compassion of Wisdom and the structure of Understanding. It is shaped into the grace of Love and fired by the discipline of Judgment. Desire becomes Beauty, Love turned outward toward a new creation, Love committed to remaking the world. It is a Love that knows the pain of death but is not defeated by it. It is a Love that dwells among us and within us. It is a Love that shines in the darkness but is not overcome by it. In the Silence and Emptiness of the tomb, the womb of Love gives birth to Beauty.

. . .

Early Christians, most notable among them Paul, speak of Jesus Christ as the "new Adam." The writer of Colossians calls him the "firstborn of all creation." Imagination suggests that, once again, God works in the Silence and Emptiness to make *tikkun,* repair. From the darkness of the tomb, Love rises, gives birth to a new creation. In the midst of the garden there awakens a new human, and a new humanity. A new hope. Beauty.

The resurrection is a new beginning. But perhaps it is only a beginning. Like *tzimtzum* and *shevirah, tikkun* is a work done in eternity. But perhaps it is done in time and place, too, and not only by Love eternally arising from the tomb but also by all those who would follow the risen one in all the moments of history. Perhaps the repair of the world is not merely to be observed but enacted, in acts of devotion and kindness, of study and discipline, of justice and mercy. Perhaps with each act the stone is rolled aside and Light of the world is freed from the darkness, and Love rises to shine with the Beauty of the Infinite. Perhaps the next act of devotion will be the one that frees the Light and consummates *tikkun.* Who knows who will do it?

Perhaps it will be you.

Shekinah—Presence

The paschal vigil is almost complete. One thing remains. The community gathers at the table on which is spread the loaf and cup of the Eucharist. Prayers are said. Bread is broken and wine poured from pitcher to chalice for all to see. Words from ancient texts and traditions are recited. "This is my body. This is my blood."

Christians of almost any persuasion believe that, in some way that may defy description, Christ is present to those who gather at the eucharistic table. That presence may be mystical— involving a transformation of the substances of bread and wine into the body and blood of Christ— or spiritual—the conviction that Christ is visible to the eyes of faith gathered at table—or symbolic—wrapped around the act of remembering Jesus' last supper with his disciples. But the enduring significance of the Eucharist is the deep sense that, gathered at the table, the Church is in the presence of Christ.

It is fitting that here, at the end of the vigil, the faithful gather around the table to experience the presence of God in Christ. This presence—*shekinah*—has been the goal of the vigil all along. The faithful wait through the night, moving gradually from hopelessness toward hope, from fear toward joy, from brokenness and alienation toward repair and redemption, always seeking the presence of God.

The paschal myth is the story of the presence of God in creation and redemption. In every reading, God is present. Present in the *bereshith* of Genesis and the story of a creation beautiful yet flawed, with the seeds of its own demise planted deep within the garden of its perfection. Present in the smoking Cloud and Fire that wreath the top of the holy mountain. Present in brokenness and healing, *shevirah* and *tikkun*, always failing, but never ceasing. Present atop the barren hill outside Jerusalem and with the lonely one crying out in his alienation and abandonment. Present in the tomb, empty and silent, where Love and Death give birth to Beauty. Present in Light shining from the realms of the Infinite. Present in the new creation. God is present, risen, moving again in the world as once again Love tries to heal a fractured creation.

There is a moment in the Eucharistic prayer at the table when the celebrant gathers the people in an act of remembering, an *anamnesis*. In its simplest form, it is the briefest of restatements of the life and death of Jesus, and the powerful transformation of his resurrection. But it is more than an act of memory, as though one recollects yesterday's breakfast or last Thursday's budget meeting. It is not merely remembering, but *re-membering*, recomposing the shattered fragments of the world, reconstituting the story of creation and redemption. It is a re-assembling of myth in the minds and hearts of those who lean on it for stability and strength, they a part of it and it a part of them. The anamnesis gathers those around the table and sets them in the midst of the story. Sets them in the presence of God. It is not that Christ was raised. It is that Christ *is risen*. It is not that Christ lived and died. It is that Christ dies and lives.

Can one imagine the vigil as an experience in anamnesis? Not as a series of moments dredged up from times long gone, but present, real, living? On this night, those who gather do not remember the story, they re-member it and dwell in it and experience it as it happens, eternally and ever and always. Creation begins in the darkness. The sea is divided. We cross holy deserts and arrive at the foot of the mountain sheathed in Fire and Cloud. We make our escape from Jericho by the slenderest of cords hung in a window. We receive the Torah from the mountain, and we forget it at the foot of the golden calf. Shattering and hope, dream and despair. Possibility and responsibility, the work of *tikkun* stretching ever on and on.

The vigil begins in darkness, outside a place hollowed out of life and emptied of possibility. The tomb is the end of failed efforts to heal the world, the death of the last hope. It is a wound in the world, a hole in the heart of God. And yet, within the hole, where all possibilities end, there is yet Possibility beyond imagining. Love moves deep within the womb of the world, the bowels of the Infinite, and slowly—as slowly as the sunrise—wells up from an abyss lost in the mists of mystery. Love rises. God is reborn. The new creation is begun.

Every year, every vigil, is an anamnesis. But so also perhaps is every night, and every sunrise. Perhaps the eternal circuit of light and dark, dark and light is not so much a changing of times as the sign that, within the Infinite, what seems to us separate is in truth united. Perhaps the myth of creation and redemption are enacted in every day, in every one of us.

Perhaps every one of us is Eve, Abraham, Isaac, Moses, Rahab, Tamar, Samuel, Mary. Perhaps every night is the womb of tomorrow, where the dawn may yet create what the night cannot imagine. Perhaps the catalogue of the day's failures as afternoon turns to dusk is but a sign that God is both persistent and merciful, impatient with what we have not done and yet eager for us to do it. Perhaps the gift of remembering is that we are re-membered, made over, reshaped, healed.

Eternally and always, the Infinite inhales, withdraws, makes a space, a hole in the heart of God. In that space, all that is not the Infinite comes into being. In that space, everything waits. The frozen caverns of the stars and the rolling canyons of the waves, the Word in the wind and the Fire in the sky, the fragments of the Light and the remnants of darkness. The hearts that yearn and the eyes that search and the ears that strain for the approach of Beauty. Creation waits in hope for *shekinah*. But not in vain. The Light is here. God is present. Christ is risen. The story begins.

Postscript

Method and Imagination

It is a delicate thing to write imaginatively about sacred texts. We assume we know them, by stint of familiarity, having long interpreted them through the application of tried and true methods, and thus have developed a benign contempt for them that permits us not to hear what they have to say. But let another risk the suggestion that perhaps our acquaintance has been inadequate, that we are no longer listening, and the hackles of self-assurance are raised.

The poems and ruminations in this book run that risk, unapologetically. They do not, however, run it alone.

First, I am blessed with patient and congenial friends who have read this book and helped give shape to its imaginings. My colleagues Cynthia L. Rigby, Lewis R. Donelson, Theodore J. Wardlaw, and Eric Wall have all been faithful and fair readers of more than one manuscript. My friend colleague David F. White deserves special thanks not only for his critical eye, but also for many hours of conversation about neo-platonism, mysticism, and theological aesthetics; I have drunk deeply from the wells of these conversations. My friends Susan Baller-Shepard, Janis Williams, Sansom Williams, and David Gambrell have also read and commented on both the poems and the ruminations herein. To all these, and to my students at Austin Presbyterian Theological Seminary who have reflected with me about poetry, theology, and imagination, I owe a debt of thanks. They bear no responsibility for errors herein contained, but without their wisdom none of this—neither truth nor error—could have come to be.

In this little book, I have drawn on many sources, most of which are sacred to someone. Hebrew and Christian Scripture, Kabbalists speculating about the origins of things, ancient neo-Platonist metaphysicians, modern Protestant theologians—I have borrowed all their voices to speak my own words. In addition, I am indebted to the thinking of such theological and liturgical scholars as John Milbank and James K. A. Smith for their work in poetics and their importance for theology and liturgy. Millbank and Smith, each in their own way, remind us that the function of theology and liturgy is *poiesis*—not merely to describe, but to *make*. I am indebted to what I understand of the work of Hans Urs von Balthasar for his understanding of art redeemed by the Incarnation. There are certainly others, perhaps some of whom I am not consciously aware, who have contributed to these poems and ruminations.

Most of all, I am indebted to the ancient rabbinical art of *midrash*, and particularly *aggadic midrash*. *Aggadah* refers to the non-legal portions of the Hebrew Scriptures, and *midrash* refers to the rabbinical style of interpretation of texts involving focus on particular words or phrases and associating with them narratives or sayings from other sources that illumine meanings not otherwise obvious. I do not claim that what I have done in this book, in either poetry or prose, is *midrash* in the truest sense. I have, however, borrowed the style of aggadic midrashists in both poem and prose. This is especially true where the interpretations have inclined in the direction of mysticism; mysticism was a common and widely drawn-upon source of commentary in aggadic midrash. The power of midrash is its ability to imagine unthought-of connections between text and larger contexts, to suggest surprising insights not anticipated by standard schools of exposition, and to engage in new conversations with old partners whose words have perhaps been forgotten or laid aside. Midrash re-enchants the text, making it newly strange.

Christianity has its own form of midrashic exegesis, in the typological interpretive methods of scholars as early as Origen, and continuing through Hilary of Poitiers, Ambrose, and Augustine. The early typologists believed that the events of the Hebrew Bible stood on their own merit as narratives (the "literal" meaning), but that there was also another "spiritual" meaning that understood them as bearing a relationship with the life of Christ. Modern biblical scholarship has looked askance at such methods, and rightly so, because they tend to "Christologize" the Hebrew Scriptures, to see their value solely to the degree that they point to Christ. Christologizing the Hebrew Scriptures is a sort of intellectual theft, depriving the text of any value as theology in its own right. But in tossing out the Christologizing bathwater, we have lost our grip on the mystical baby. A part of what I have sought to do in these pages is not to evacuate the stories of the Hebrew Scriptures of their meaning, but to lay them alongside the traditions of Christian theology, and to allow the two mutually to inform each other. I have sought to imagine them into a grand conversation about creation, life, redemption, and the presence of God.

Imagination has the power to re-enchant theology, a power desperately needed in this day of reductionism, when truth is reduced to congruence with existing worldview and equated with facts as they are accepted by the speaker. Imagination re-enchants theology by liberating it from the prison of proof, infusing doctrine with poetic capacity for flight, and releasing it to fly free in a universe of its own creation. Imagination summons new partners into the conversation, hears old words with new ears. Imagination makes the familiar newly strange.

Samuel Taylor Coleridge thought carefully about imagination in his *Biographia Literaria*. For Coleridge, the problem with his own age (and how much more so in our own!) was the assumption that the mind is a passive receptor of perceived data from the senses, a sort of computer into which "facts" are input and from which "truth" was produced. Coleridge was horrified by this thinking and proposed instead that the mind is nothing less than the human capacity to imitate the creativity of God. Coleridge spoke of two forms of imagination. The first was "Primary Imagination," which for Coleridge was the "living Power and prime Agent of all human Perception, as a repetition in the finite mind of the eternal act of creation in the infinite I AM." And "Secondary Imagination" was

> "an echo of the former, co-existing with the conscious will . . . . It dissolves, diffuses, dissipates, in order to re-create; or where this process is rendered impossible, yet still at all events it struggles to idealize and to unify. It is essentially *vital*, even as all objects are essentially fixed and dead."[1]

Coleridge understands the human mind as a "primary Agent" engaged in creating new reality, not merely a stenographer recording information. Our capacity of Primary Imagination enables us to imagine that which does not exist (an imitation of divine creativity), and our Secondary Imagination— the imagination of the poet, artist, musician, and, I believe, theologian— empowers us to "dissolve, diffuse, dissipate in order to re-create" that reality in art. Our Primary Imagination bears us on flights through the universe of divine Possibility. Our Secondary Imagination interprets and digests those flights into vision that we can share with one another.

---

1. Samuel Taylor Coleridge, *Biographia Literaria, I.* ed. J. Engell and W. Jackson Bate. Princeton: Princeton University Press, 1983, pp 304.

In these poems and ruminations, I have tried to live out what Coleridge describes. The Scriptural texts and liturgical movements of the paschal vigil have been the launching point for flights of imaginative fancy, overflying aspects of mysticism and science and doctrinal theology. I have first lived those flights and then tried to interpret them in words, both poetic and prosaic. My hope is that, in an alchemy I neither understand nor control, these words have given wings to the imagination of the reader, and allowed it to soar, as well.